AQA BUSINESS STUDIES for AS
REVISION GUIDE SECOND EDITION

Ian Marcousé
Marie Brewer
Andrew Hammond

Orders: please contact Bookpoint Ltd, 130 Milton Park, Abingdon, Oxon OX14 4SB.
Telephone: (44) 01235 827720. Fax: (44) 01235 400454. Lines are open from 9.00–5.00,
Monday to Saturday, with a 24 hour message answering service. You can also order through
our website www.hoddereducation.co.uk

If you have any comments to make about this, or any of our other titles, please send them
to educationenquiries@hodder.co.uk

British Library Cataloguing in Publication Data
A catalogue record for this title is available from the British Library

ISBN: 978 1 444 10796 8

First Edition Published 2005
This Edition Published 2010
Impression number 10 9 8 7 6 5 4 3 2 1
Year   2014 2013 2012 2011 2010

Hachette UK's policy is to use papers that are natural, renewable and
recyclable products and made from wood grown in sustainable forests.
The logging and manufacturing processes are expected to conform to the
environmental regulations of the country of origin.

Cover illustration © Oxford Illustrators and Designers
Typeset by Phoenix Photosetting, Chatham, Kent
Printed in Italy for Hodder Education, an Hachette UK Company, 338 Euston Road,
London NW1 3BH

Contents

Introduction

This revision book is written to help push every reader's AS results up by at least one grade. It does this by focusing the AS subject content on the exam skills sought by examiners. The writing style is analytic, but applied to the context of real businesses, just as the examiners want. Every chapter points out key evaluative themes within the syllabus. As knowledge of the syllabus counts for only one-third of the marks at AS level, revision must do more than re-hash facts and definitions. This Revision Guide teaches the reader to develop all the exam skills needed for success.

Each unit within the book covers a different section of the AS specification. All the key concepts are explained, with the more difficult ones getting longer, fuller explanations. The content is full of references to real firms and application is further enhanced by dedicated sections in each unit. There are also questions to test yourself in every unit. The answers are set out at the back of the book to provide immediate feedback on how your revision is going.

Also remember the Revision Checklists at the back of the book, which are written to help you revise thoughtfully.

In addition to this book, it is hugely helpful to:
- Use the actual and 'specimen' exam papers available at **www.aqa.com**
- Go through the Specification content, word by word, using the *A-Z Business Studies Handbook*, Philip Allan 2009 as your companion. This book will be invaluable for your A2 studies and is widely used by 1st year university students – so your money will not be wasted
- Regularly read articles from *Business Review* magazine. It will be available in your school/ college library. Look out especially for articles by Andrew Gillespie, Ian Marcousé, Malcolm Surridge and John Wolinski.

The authors

Ian Marcousé has devised the format of the book and edited all the text and questions. Ian is the Chair of Examiners for a major exam board and a leading author. He is also the founding editor of *Business Review* magazine.

Marie Brewer is an experienced author and a Senior Examiner for a major exam board.

Andrew Hammond is an experienced author, a regular contributor to *Business Review* and a Senior Examiner for a major exam board. He is also Head of Business Studies at Darrick Wood School, Bromley.

1 Starting a business

Unit 1   Enterprise and entrepreneurs

What?

Enterprise is the collection of skills that make a business idea happen. It is also used as an alternative word for a business. Entrepreneurs are the people who turn business ideas into reality.

At each stage of the process *value is added*. The price of the basic ingredients often bears little resemblance to the final price to the consumer. The beans in the £2 cup of coffee would have been bought for less than 1p. This process of adding value is what makes enterprise worthwhile. The *added value* contributes to the profit that the enterprise makes.

The economy is described as having different sectors. These are:

- *Primary* – growing, fishing, mining and extracting raw materials. In many developing countries this sector accounts for most of the economic activity. In the UK it is less than 2 per cent.
- *Secondary* – this is basically manufacturing but includes engineering and construction. It is the sector that turns raw materials into finished, packaged goods. Traditionally it is the sector where the most value is added.
- *Tertiary* – this is the service sector. It includes selling, both wholesalers and retailers, as well as financial services, media, and the countless other business services. This is the largest sector in the UK economy.

Some businesses may be in more than one sector. A farmer selling farm produce has grown the vegetables (primary) and then sells to the public (tertiary). If he also makes and sells yoghurt then he is also in the secondary sector. Other businesses may be in just one. Most of the new business start-ups in the UK are in the tertiary sector. This may be because it is easier to start a sole trader business providing services than to start a manufacturing process that requires space, machinery and people.

Who?

Entrepreneurs come in many shapes and forms. They are not all whizz-kids or big names such as Richard Branson. Many successful businesses are started by people who never hit the headlines. One in six new businesses are started by people over fifty.

In order to make a business idea succeed entrepreneurs need to be:

- *Willing to take a risk* – a new business venture almost always carries a risk. There are very few certainties when starting a new business. Even a perfect idea may hit snags such as the onset of recession or a change in taste or a rival getting to the market sooner. If the idea fails it will result in a loss of capital, the time invested will be wasted and there may well be a loss of reputation.
- *Determined* – most new businesses will face problems. A strong determination to 'make it happen' will be invaluable. Having a passion for the product will make them push through difficulties.
- *Have persuasive abilities* – most business ideas need some form of external support. Being able to convince others to lend money or to support your venture can be vital.
- *Good at building relationships* – most businesses need to be involved with other organisations or people. Suppliers, workers, customers all need to be dealt with and if relationships are good it can help to solve problems if they occur.

However

If a business is to succeed the personal qualities of the entrepreneur may not be enough.

- *Market research is vital* – the entrepreneur needs to know if the product or service will sell and if there is competition from alternative products or businesses.
- *It also needs good business planning* – the best idea in the world may fail if there is insufficient finance available. If the marketing is insufficient, customers may be unaware of the product or service.
- *Timing is also important* – starting a business during an economic downturn is clearly going to be more difficult than during a boom time.

Why?

There are many reasons why new businesses are started. Those started by the over-fifties could well be as a result of redundancy. The prospect of getting a new job is greatly reduced so people look to going it alone. Others may be the result of a change of direction – doing something you have always wanted to do. For some people a business grows from an idea. Maybe they spot a gap in a market. Several have been started by mums who found it difficult to get something for their children, so set up a business to supply to others.

Profit?

It is a common assumption that entrepreneurs are 'in it for the money'. Of course making money is important but it is rarely the prime motivation for a business venture. Many people just want to be their own boss. Others have a passion for a particular idea.

That does not mean that profit is not important. Even the most passionate entrepreneur cannot keep supporting a business idea that is constantly making a loss. Profit gives a return for the time, effort and finance invested in the business. Without some return external funding will be impossible. If the business is to grow it will also need profit so that there is money to reinvest in the business.

Profit is the reward for the risk that the entrepreneur takes when starting up a new business.

Opportunity cost

When someone starts a business they have to give up doing something else. The money they invest cannot be used to buy a new car. Their time cannot be spent doing other things. This concept – the cost of what is being given up in order to do something – is known as *opportunity cost*.

As resources are limited choices have to be made. When a person sets up a new business one of the opportunity costs to them may be the loss of their salary in the previous job. Apart from the money, they may also be giving up a secure income for a more risky future. The satisfaction of setting up the enterprise may well be balanced by the increased risk. One of the features of entrepreneurs is that they are willing to take the risk.

What is risk?

All new businesses carry some degree of risk. The newer or more innovative the idea the greater the risk of failure will be. Even with established ideas there is still risk. Maybe there is too much competition or maybe competitors act aggressively towards the new

Exam insight ....

Be careful not to get too excited by the apparent success of a young entrepreneur. In the exam carefully analyse which factors contributed to the success of the business. Was it a good idea at the right time? Was it good planning and careful management? The reasons for business success are very varied. Be sure to discuss the issues that are relevant to the circumstances.

start-up. Maybe fashion will change. An economic downturn would change the business environment and so make it harder to succeed.

Managing risk

The secret is to try to minimise the amount of risk. It is often said that entrepreneurs take a 'calculated risk'. This means that they know the level of risk and have decided that they can live with this and so are prepared to have a go. Business Angels, who provide funding to new and growing businesses, know that not every business will succeed. They hope to make enough return from the successes to cover the loss from the failures. They are balancing the risk.

Calculating the level of risk requires good research. This will give a good understanding of the market and can help to identify things that could go wrong. It may then be possible to take steps to minimise the problems and so effectively reduce the degree of risk.

Themes for evaluation

The image of entrepreneurs is dominated by people such as Peter Jones, Theo Paphitis and Richard Branson. However, the majority of new business start-ups are done quietly by very ordinary people who have a good idea or see a gap in the market and have the determination to make it work. It is also worth remembering that not all businesses succeed. The reasons for a business success can be very varied – a good idea, hard work, good planning or maybe occasionally just good luck.

Key terms

Business plan – a statement of the business plans for the future; what it hopes to achieve and how it will go about doing that

External finance – money invested in the business from sources outside the business

Profit – the return made by the business after all costs have been deducted

Test yourself

1 List two qualities an entrepreneur might have. (2)
2 Explain the differences between the different sectors of the economy. (9)
3 What is meant by opportunity cost? Give an example. (4)
4 Why is profitability important? (4)
5 What is meant by calculated risk? (2)
6 What does someone setting up a new business need to do before starting out? (4)

Unit 2 Identifying business opportunities

AQA Business Studies for AS Revision Guide

What?

A business opportunity is a possibility of starting up a new business or introducing a new product into the market. Successful entrepreneurs seize the opportunity and get into the market before others.

Why?

The interests of the person starting the business often generate new business ideas. A cycling fanatic may start a bicycle repair shop. A young mother with a small baby may find that she is unable to buy something that she needs so may start up a business to fill that need. An inventor may come up with a new product so will start a business to manufacture and sell it.

Others want to start their own business so will look around for a gap in the market or come up with a new business idea. Some entrepreneurs introduce an idea that has worked in another country.

Which?

New business ideas come in many forms:
- They may fill a gap in a local market – there is no Indian restaurant in this town. A seaside resort may have many ice cream stalls but there may be a gap in the market for an ice cream parlour where customers can sit and eat their ice creams.
- They may satisfy a niche. Parking is readily available at UK airports but some firms have introduced a valet service where the traveller is met at departure and the car taken to a car park and then brought back to arrivals when the traveller returns. This is an expensive alternative but satisfies a niche in the market.
- They may be based on a new way to sell an existing product or service. The internet has seen a growth of many new businesses selling products traditionally only available on the High Street. Glasses Direct sells prescription glasses directly to the customer using the internet. 'A Quarter Of' is an online old-fashioned sweet shop.

How?

Spotting a business opportunity may be a matter of chance or luck but there are tools that can be used.

- Researching existing markets is an obvious way to see if there is a gap in the market. A useful tool for this is *market mapping*. This defines the key features of the market and then matches that with existing products or businesses within the market. This is then drawn up on a diagram and any gaps can be seen.
- Brainstorming involves coming up with ideas however ridiculous they may seem. Hopefully one of the ideas will work.
- Researching future markets: by looking at likely changes to society, fashion or the economy new business ideas may be found. The growth in the number of older people has meant new business opportunities in providing for this segment of the market. An economic downturn may mean that there is an opportunity to introduce a cheaper alternative to existing products.

What then?

Once the entrepreneur has come up with a business idea it is important to research the idea before starting up. The business needs to know if there is a market for the product and what is the nature of any competition.

As a new business it is unlikely that funds will be available for full-scale market research. However research is vital. Depending on the type of business, *small-scale research* can be done. If the business is selling to other businesses then talking to those businesses may give an idea of how well the product will be received. A High Street business can check out the number of passers-by and look to see what competition is in the neighbourhood and what prices similar outlets are charging. A new product can be tried out on family and friends before launching to the general public.

Exam insight

When answering a question about new business success or failure, look very carefully to see why this business succeeded. Think about business theory. Was there a gap in the market? Was the product innovative or differentiated in some way from existing products? Was the business start-up well planned? Was the marketing effective? But remember to look at other factors. Did the entrepreneur have any special qualities? Was it a case of being in the right place at the right time? Did they spot a business opportunity and act on it?

Franchising

Not everyone starts a business completely from scratch. One of the ways of getting into business is to take on a *franchise*. This means buying the right to use the name and trading methods of an existing business.

When a business idea has been successful in one location, the owner can choose to finance setting up more stores, or sell the rights to franchisees. From its origins with one sandwich shop, Fred de Luca's Subway chain now has more than 32,000 stores. A fee is paid for the franchise and training is given. The person taking on the franchise has to run the business in exactly the same way as the master business. For a Subway sandwich shop, for example, that will mean the same products, the same layout and same branding.

The advantages of a franchise are:

- The idea has already been tested. Banks say that franchise start-ups are less likely to fail. Over 90 per cent of franchises survive for over three years as compared to 70 per cent of all new start-ups.
- For the original owner (the franchisor) it is a way of expanding the business without having to worry about running every outlet.
- The franchisee gets a tried and tested business idea.
- It is easier to obtain external funding for a franchise than for a completely new business.

The disadvantages are:

- The franchisor only gets part of the profits from the business.
- A poor franchisee may damage the business concept.
- The franchisees do not have total control. They have to run the business as outlined in the franchise agreement.

Support

Help for people who are setting up a new business is very varied. The Government's main service for new businesses is Business Link. It runs a website that offers advice to people wishing to set up a business and provides links to other organisations that may be able to offer either financial help or advice. Many local authorities also provide help and advice to would-be entrepreneurs. Most banks offer a service to help new business start-ups. This mainly consists of help with the preparation of business plans. Some organisations will offer mentoring. This is where an experienced businessperson will give guidance and support to someone starting out.

There are also schemes such as the Prince's Trust that help young people to start up businesses.

Application

From reggae artist to millionaire

The story of Levi Roots is a modern day success story. The 'Reggae Reggae' sauce that has made him rich and famous was based on a recipe handed down from his grandmother. It was initially made by him and his family in their kitchen and sold at a London street market. Following his appearance on Dragon's Den a deal was struck with Sainsbury's. It rapidly became one of their fastest selling products. Since then Levi has expanded his range of products, opened a restaurant, written a cookery book and become a TV chef.

So what was the secret of his success?

A good product – financial backing – excellent publicity – the entrepreneur's personality. All of these together have contributed but you can't help wondering if the real break was when a talent scout for the Dragon's Den programme spotted him. Luck perhaps?

Themes for evaluation

Starting up a business is a challenging experience. Coming up with new ideas can vary from the flash in the pan through to the result of careful planning and research. There is no magic bullet for having a successful business but analysts would all agree that good research backed up by careful planning are vital ingredients. Often it looks as if luck plays a big part, but luck is usually helped along by determination and good planning.

Key terms

Franchisee – a person who takes on a franchise
Franchisor – the owner of the franchise idea
Niche – a small part of a larger market

Test yourself

1 What is meant by a gap in the market? (2)
2 What is a niche market? (2)
3 How can an entrepreneur with limited resources conduct market research? (4)
4 List two advantages of taking up a franchise. (4)
5 How does the Government help people to start up new businesses? (2)
6 Why do they do this? (4)

Identifying business opportunities

Unit 3 Protecting business ideas

What?

A new business idea is difficult to protect, as it is often difficult to define. *Intellectual property* is a general term used to define original creative ideas. It applies to music, writing, engineering, and photography. If there was no way to stop people copying, authors, composers and inventors would be less likely to come up with new ideas.

How?

The Intellectual Property Office – the IPO – is the government office that deals with the legal protection of business ideas. There are three main areas where legal protection can be obtained. These are:

Copyright

This applies to all written work and to sound and film recordings. It allows authors, composers and inventors to prevent others from copying their work. This is why you cannot legally photocopy a book or download music on the internet without paying for it.

Patents

A patent allows for an original idea to be protected for a period of 20 years. In order to protect the invention, a patent has to be applied for. This process can take several years to complete as the Patent Office needs to be sure that the invention is original.

Trademark

A trademark is defined as 'any sign that distinguishes the goods and services of one trader from those of another'. It may be a logo or a name or a style of packaging or a taste or smell. There are several iconic trademarks such as those for Coca-Cola and Apple. These enable the customer to instantly recognise the product. A business can register its trademark so that anyone who copies the logo can be sued. To be registered it must be distinctive.

Why?

Without protecting intellectual property, there would be no point in Apple investing billions of dollars in research and development into ever-better music, phone and computing products. Nor would authors have an incentive to write books. Protection means that they can sell these ideas and so get a return for their efforts.

A trademark helps to distinguish a product or service so that customers can easily recognise and remember it and hopefully make a repeat purchase. For some products with well-known trademarks it adds considerable value. Not only does it encourage people to buy the product – think Nike trainers or Cadbury's chocolate – but it also means that the company can charge a premium for the product.

But

The downside is that, if inventions cannot be copied, the owner of the idea has a monopoly and can therefore charge the customer higher prices. There is considerable debate about the prices charged by drug companies. Some argue that drugs ought to be available cheaply to those who need them (for example AIDS drugs in Africa). The drug companies argue that without the high prices they charge for new drugs there would be no research and therefore no medical breakthroughs.

Who?

Any person or business obtains copyright on their original written work (automatically), and can register a trademark or patent an idea. Inventors must patent their ideas before bringing them to the market to ensure that they are the owners of the invention. A small new business such as a window cleaner or plumber is unlikely to register a trademark initially. For one thing it is additional expense, typically over £1000. However if the business takes off and they look to expand and perhaps franchise the business then they will almost certainly want to register the company name or logo.

Does it work?

It has become increasingly difficult to protect business ideas. The growth of the internet means that it is much easier to copy and distribute material without the owner's permission. It is very hard to police the downloading of items such as music tracks. There have been some prosecutions that may have put people off, but it is still common practice.

Another problem is that very few products or services are so different from rivals that it is possible to protect them. Think of the number of branded coffee shops in town centres. Is Starbucks really that different from Costa Coffee?

Another way?

Getting legal protection for an idea or a trademark is one way of keeping competition at bay. However a better way is to make the product or service so desirable that the customer will choose it. Building a product **brand** will promote customer loyalty and make sales easier. It is true that Nike has registered their trademark 'tick' but the brand itself is what sells the goods. However, even branded goods can have problems.

One problem is fake goods. They are usually of much lower quality and so can damage the firm's reputation. Large international businesses spend considerable sums trying to prevent the production and selling of these fake goods.

Protecting business ideas also does not guarantee business success. A poor idea will not sell no matter how well protected.

Application

When Vernon Kerswell appeared on Dragon's Den his request for funding for his business Extreme Flier Toys was turned down because of worries that he might not be able to get patents for his toys. The 21-year-old inventor wanted to swap 15 per cent of his business for an investment of £75,000. He started the business after a visit to China where he saw a factory producing toys. After suggesting some modifications he came back with the toys which he started selling while still a student. The 'Dragons' appeared to like his toys and were very encouraging but declined to invest, as they did not think that Vernon would be able to patent his products. Since the show was recorded Vernon has had his patents confirmed and one of the 'Dragons' has been in touch to offer to get involved with the business. Now the business looks set to prosper with confirmed orders worth over £100,000.

Themes for evaluation

Having a well-known trademark can undoubtedly add value to a product and an inventor or creative person needs to protect their ideas. However for most businesses there is no advantage to be gained from applying for legal protection. Starbucks as an international chain of coffee shops will have registered its trademark, but for the fish and chip shop in the town there is nothing to be gained. For most businesses the main issue is not legal protection but finding ways of distinguishing themselves or their product from competitors. The fish and chip shop has to get a reputation for serving the best fish and chips in order to keep attracting customers. The plumbing firm has to do a good job so that people will ask them back and recommend them to their friends.

For many businesses, product differentiation is more important than legal protection.

Key terms

Branded product – a product or service that has a distinctive feature that enables it to be instantly recognised

Monopoly – a market where there is only one seller of a product or service

Product differentiation – making a product stand out in the market

Test yourself

1 How do authors and composers benefit from copyright on their work? (4)
2 With the growth of the internet why has it become more difficult to protect copyrighted material? (4)
3 How does a trademark help a business? (6)
4 Why might a patent be bad for consumers? (4)
5 Do you agree with the drug company's argument that they need to charge high prices to pay back the research costs? (8)
6 How does protecting your business idea reduce the risk involved in setting up a business? (6)

Protecting business ideas

Unit 4 Developing business plans

What?

A business plan is a document stating the objectives for a business and how they will be achieved. It is designed to provide enough financial and other information about a business to persuade backers to invest in the business. A business plan should contain the answers to all the questions a 'Dragon' investor might pose.

Why?

There are three key purposes for producing a business plan:

1 *To gain finance.* Any banker or investor will want to see a well drawn up business plan. It should show and justify key data such as a cash flow forecast. This will enable investors to make their own judgement about the risks they will be taking before they part with their cash.
2 *To clarify the idea.* The process of constructing a detailed plan forces the entrepreneur to think about what differentiates the business, what is needed to get it going and how likely it is to succeed.
3 *To monitor success.* Once the business is up and running, the firm's performance can be measured by referring back to its financial and sales forecasts.

Who?

All new businesses would benefit from preparing a business plan. If external finance is needed the lender will require a business plan to be prepared before they will consider lending. Even if there is no need for external funding a business plan will help to clarify the business idea and to ensure that everything has been thought about.

There will be obvious differences of approach depending on the type of business. A business support service run from home will have very different plans to a manufacturing business which will need a factory site, machinery and skilled staff.

Manufacturing start-ups will focus on the details of the production equipment and machinery required. Skills of staff may be more important than in the service sector, so personnel issues such as recruitment and training may be crucial.

A service sector business plan is more likely to focus on marketing elements – in particular in stressing a unique selling point to the service.

What's in it?

- Introduction: a brief description of the business idea and why it should be a success. It should outline the existing market and identify the gap the new business can fit into.
- Personal information: the entrepreneurs' qualifications, experience, skills and financial position.
- Objectives: what the business hopes to achieve, in the first year, but also in the medium term.
- Marketing plan: should answer questions such as: Who are the customers? Who are the competitors? How big is our market? What is special about our product/service? What will our marketing strategy be?
- Production plan: what is needed in terms of space, equipment, raw materials and staff? How can these be obtained? Who will do which tasks and when?
- Financial plan: cash flow forecast, a break-even calculation and information on the sources of finance and the capital or collateral being offered by the owners (for example, outside investors would be impressed by someone willing to use their own house as collateral for a loan).

What it does and doesn't do

It does	It does not
Boost chances of success because it makes the entrepreneur think through the ideas and processes	Guarantee success
Involve detailed financial forecasts	Mean that the forecasts will be accurate. They will only be estimates
Form the basis of a budgeting system	Work as the basis of a budgeting system unless it allows for flexibility
Take a significant amount of time and effort to create	Mean a waste of time – planning may throw up previously unforeseen problems
Help to persuade others to invest in the business	Ensure that external funding will be obtained

Application

The television programme *Dragon's Den* has brought the concept of starting a business into the living room. We are all familiar with the parade of would-be entrepreneurs who put forward their quirky ideas before the would-be lenders. What is very obvious is that the 'Dragons' want to see that the idea has been well thought out. They heap derision on the poor person who has no idea how many they are likely to sell or how much money they might make. Almost without exception, the ones who succeed in persuading the 'Dragons' to invest have a good idea backed by test marketing and well-constructed financial information. In other words they have a business plan.

Themes for evaluation

Is there any point in spending time constructing a business plan when much of it is based on guesswork?

If external finance is necessary the lending institutions will demand a business plan before even granting an appointment let alone lending money. Where no external finance is needed enterprises are often started informally and without a business plan. Many of them succeed, however it is likely that many of the new businesses that fail might have been better equipped to deal with problems had they prepared a business plan. Planning does help to increase the chances of success. A carefully constructed plan will take time, effort and research but should flag up potential problems so that these can be planned for.

Does a business plan guarantee success?

No, there are too many uncontrollable external factors such as competition and changing consumer tastes. The plan is no guarantee, but it increases the chance of success.

Key terms

Collateral – assets used to provide security on a loan, e.g. an entrepreneur may use their home as collateral for a business start-up loan

Entrepreneur – a risk taker; the person willing to put in the time, effort and money to set up and run their own business

Exam insight

Most questions relating to business planning will be evaluative questions requiring some form of judgement as to the merits of the planning process. All too often answers can be one-sided, either concentrating on the positives of planning (e.g. helps to ensure success, etc.) or on the limitations of planning. In reality, business planning is a useful process with accepted limitations. Effective judgements will consider the validity of the plan in question. This will be dependent upon a number of factors, including:

- the experience of the person constructing the plan and their market knowledge;
- the time and care that has gone into the research upon which the plan is based;
- the level of competition in the market in which the business is operating.

Test yourself

1 Identify the five key sections of a business plan. (5)
2 Why do banks and other lenders insist on seeing a business plan before deciding whether or not to lend to the business? (4)
3 Even if external finance is not needed why might constructing a business plan be a good idea? (4)
4 Why is it a good idea to review the plan after the business has been operating for a year? (4)

Unit 5   Choosing the right legal structure

Legally, business organisations can be classified in a number of different ways. The most important feature of these different types of organisation is the liability of the owner for any debts incurred by the business. The owners of sole traders and almost all partnerships have what is known as unlimited liability. This means that business debts have to be paid out of personal or family funds or assets (you could lose your house); owners (shareholders) of both private and public limited companies are protected by limited liability.

What?

Sole traders

A sole trader is a personal business, owned and run by one person. In law, there is no financial separation between the person and the business, so any debts incurred by the business are personal debts of the owner. The owner's personal assets can therefore be lost in order to cover debts run up by the business.

Why be a sole trader?	Why not?
Complete lack of formalities	Unlimited liability
Easy to set up	Big problems if owner is ill or away
Owner in complete control	Lack of finance (and banks may be less willing to lend to a sole trader than larger firms)

Application

Sole traders are characterised by a massive time commitment on behalf of the owner, a shortage of available sources of finance and very often confusion between personal and business issues. Sole traders frequently fail to account for their own wages, so rely on the ability of their business to produce profit in order for them to live. In the event of the business failing the owner may lose personal assets in order to satisfy the creditors of the firm (those to whom money is owed).

Partnerships

A partnership shares a key feature with sole traders – that of unlimited liability for the owners. In the case of a partnership, however, there is more than one owner of the business. The partners draw up a partnership agreement stating who owns how much of the firm, who has invested what and how much of the profit goes to each partner.

Why form a partnership?	Why not?
Complete lack of formalities	Unlimited liability
Extra owners share the risk	Big problems if a partner dies or is simply away
New partners can bring in extra capital	All partners are bound by one partner's actions on behalf of the business (e.g. if debts are incurred)
New partners may bring specialist skills	Potential for disagreements between partners

What next?

The next step is incorporation, to become a private limited company. This means that the business is given its own legal status, separate from that of its owners. This therefore means that business debts are not the owners' personal debts. As a result, the owners of a company with limited liability can only lose the money they have invested in the business.

Exam insight

Business start-ups will be sole traders, partnerships or private limited companies. The BUSS1 exam you take will be focused on one particular business, so look carefully at the case study to check which type of business the entrepreneur has decided to use. If the letters Ltd follow the company name, you are dealing with a private limited company. If they are not there, the firm is either a sole trader or partnership – in which case, the owner(s) have unlimited liability.

Application of limited liability to manufacturing versus service businesses

Limited liability is vital when setting up a manufacturing firm of any size. The investments required for machinery and equipment, along with the cost of buying materials and other supplies, mean that a manufacturer may well build up substantial debts before receiving any revenue. In such cases the ability to limit the risks faced by the owners is critical to encourage them to risk setting up the firm. By contrast, many service firms can be set up relatively cheaply, with little need for substantial investment in plant and machinery.

Another what

Private limited company

A private limited company (with the letters Ltd after its name) is the simplest form of limited liability company. Its key feature, after the limited liability of its owners, is the need for the shareholders to agree to any transfer in ownership of the business' shares. This, in reality, limits the potential shareholders and therefore the potential for a private limited company to generate equity capital.

Why be Ltd?	Why not?
Owners have limited liability	Accounts must be publicly available at Companies' House
Greater scope for raising capital than sole traders/partnerships	Other formalities, such as holding an annual general meeting (AGM) must be observed
Shareholders retain control over who owns shares (unlike plcs)	Still limited potential for raising share capital

Public limited company

Public limited companies (denoted by the letters plc in the name) are companies that are allowed to sell their shares on the stock exchange. This means that these companies have the potential to raise significantly higher sums of capital through the sale of shares, meaning that, generally, plcs are the largest firms within the UK.

Why be plc?	Why not?
Access to vast amounts of capital through the stock market	Stock market demands may cause over-emphasis on short-term objectives
Enhanced reputation	Potential for takeover
Likely to find borrowing easier and cheaper	Greater administration costs, both during and after flotation

Themes for evaluation

Risk

Crucial to the concept of limited liability (the major issue in this unit) is the idea of the risks involved in starting up in business. Limiting the liability of company owners allows those owners to take the kinds of risks that allow firms to grow and operate on a large and more efficient scale. However, limiting the liability of owners has a flip-side. Companies can be formed that run up huge debts, financing the huge expense accounts of directors before going into liquidation. The result is that shareholders lose only the amount of money they originally invested, whereas creditors are left with bad debts that will never be repaid.

Short-termism in public limited companies

A charge levelled at some firms listed on the stock market is that they take decisions designed to maximise the short-term profits of the firm (thus keeping share prices high), at the cost of the long-term success of the firm.

Key Terms

Limited liability – the liability of the owners of private and public limited companies is limited to the amount they have invested in the business
Short-termism – a tendency to focus on achieving short-term objectives, often at the cost of long-term success
Unlimited liability – a situation where the owner of a business is personally liable for any debts incurred by the business

Test yourself

1 Explain three issues that a pair of entrepreneurs may consider when discussing whether to start up as a partnership or a private limited company. (6)
2 Identify three differences between a private and a public limited company. (3)
3 Briefly explain why you may be more likely to be ripped off by a private limited company than a partnership. (3)
4 Outline two benefits of starting up a café as a sole trader. (4)
5 List four reasons why some private limited companies choose not to become public. (4)

Choosing the right legal structure

2 Getting the start-up right

Unit 6 Market research

What?

Market research is the process of gathering information so that a firm can understand its market. Market research gathers information about customers, competitors and distributors.

Which?

All businesses will benefit from understanding their market.

- Small local firms such as a hairdresser or butcher will have direct knowledge of their customers and competitors so may not need to conduct any formal research. If they wish to expand or to introduce new products, market research will be helpful in avoiding costly mistakes.
- Large firms with a wide portfolio of products will need to be constantly researching their markets. They may have a wealth of information about existing products and markets but may still do research to see what would happen if the product was modified or if the price was changed.
- Businesses supplying other firms (*business to business*) may have less need of market research if they are providing products or services to customer specifications.

For a **new business** market research is essential. A new business has no knowledge of the market. It has not tested itself or its products in the marketplace, so has no definite information about how customers will react to its products or services. Understanding the market will help a new business to reduce its risks.

What?

One of the difficulties that a business start-up has is knowing what it needs to know. In order to build a business plan it will need to have some idea of the demand for its product.

- *Market size*

  A good place to start is the size of the market. If it is an existing market then it will be possible to find out how large the total market is. If it is a new product or service then a starting point is the number of people who might be interested.

- *Market share*

  Based on the total market available the firm will then want to estimate how much of that market might be available to them. This will need knowledge of competitors and how strong they are in the market.

How?

Researchers gather information either by using information that already exists (**secondary** or **desk research**) or by going out into the market to gather first-hand information (**primary** or **field research**).

Methods of secondary research

This uses data that already exist. It is therefore easier and cheaper than conducting primary research. It is available from many sources such as:

- *Market intelligence reports*: these are prepared by organisations such as Keynotes, Mintel and Retail Business (EIU). They collect a vast range of data on markets and give valuable analysis of trends that they sell to interested parties.
- *Government statistics*: government departments collect and publish a wealth of statistics relating to population and economic activity.
- *Internet*: internet search engines such as Google can provide links to a vast range of information.

Methods of primary research

This is the process of gathering information *directly* from the market.

- It can be tailored very specifically to the product or business.
- Firms can identify buying patterns and changes in customer behaviour.

Several methods are available to business start-ups.

- Talking directly to potential customers is useful for getting customer ideas.
- Observation – how many people pass a potential site? What are customers buying in similar outlets?
- Talking to other retailers. They have the closest contact with customers.

A business start-up may well be able to do most of this research itself. If the research is more complicated then it may pay to use a *market research agency*.

Quantitative and qualitative research

Most market research is *quantitative* – that is it gives numerical information: 10,000 people live within four miles of a shop site; sales of bicycles last year were 1.2 million, up 13 per cent since the previous year.

Qualitative research looks at the psychological reasons why people make buying decisions.

Qualitative research

This is most likely to be primary research. Two main approaches are used:
- *Group discussions*
  Sometimes called focus groups. Group members are asked to focus on a particular topic such as the taste or name of a product. This can help to:
  - reveal problems or opportunities
  - tell the firm why customers are making certain choices.
- *In-depth interviews*
  These are usually conducted on a similar basis to group discussions but on a one-to-one basis so they avoid the problems of members of the group being influenced by others.

Questionnaires

Questionnaires are a commonly used tool for collecting both quantitative and qualitative market information. They ask preset questions of a sample of people. They need to be properly designed if they are to be of any value. The key features of a *good questionnaire* are:
- questions do not lead towards a particular answer;
- questions are clear and unambiguous;
- questions will include basic demographic information, thus enabling a better analysis of the results.

Another important consideration with question–naires is the *response rate*. Traditionally postal questionnaires have a low response, which may lead to biased results. Face-to-face questionnaires have a much higher response rate but are expensive and the business needs to balance cost and effectiveness.

Why?

Why is it important to get the sample right?

Questionnaires are based on samples. It is too expensive to ask the whole population. The art of sampling is to get a good representative sample.
1 *Sampling method*: this can affect the validity of the sample. There are three main sampling methods:
   - random sampling, which involves picking the sample at random (e.g. by picking every fiftieth person);

- quota sampling, where the people used for the sample are chosen to represent the profile of the target market. If, for example, 20 per cent of the target market is of the under-18 age group, then 20 out of a sample of 100 will have to be under-18;
- stratified sampling, in which one important feature of the target market is identified, then the whole sample is based on that feature, e.g. KitKat Senses is mainly bought by women, so a stratified sample would be women-only.
2 *Sample size*: the sample has to be large enough to ensure that it is valid. Generally samples of about 200–1000 are considered large enough to reflect opinions accurately. Firms often use smaller samples because of the cost of research on this scale.

Exam insight

Remember that market research is not just about questionnaires.

When answering a question about market research, take care to focus your answer on the particular business. Ask yourself: 'What does the business need to know?' Then think about how it should go about getting the information. A broad sweeping answer will not get you any application or analysis marks.

Evaluation

The extent to which companies, especially larger businesses, have come to rely on market research is often criticised. Yet there is little doubt that an understanding of customer behaviour helps a business to produce products the market wants. With a start-up business, market research is essential. It reduces risk and may help to avoid a disastrous failure. Like many other business tools, market research needs to be cost effective.

Key Terms

Market research agency – a business that specialises in conducting market research
Target market – the section of the population that the firm wants to sell to

Test yourself

1 Why is it particularly important for a business start-up to conduct market research? (4)
2 Explain the difference between primary and secondary research. (4)
3 What is the difference between quantitative and qualitative research? (4)
4 Identify two disadvantages of random sampling and two of quota sampling. (4)
5 Outline two factors affecting how large a sample size a firm would want to use. (4)
6 What do you need to do to design a good questionnaire? (4)

Unit 7 Understanding markets

What?

A market is where buyers and sellers get together in order to exchange goods and services. When a business talks about the market it means its customers and factors such as the economy and competition that affect customer behaviour. In order to sell to the customer a business needs to have knowledge of this market. With good market knowledge a business can have the right products in the right place at the right time, promoted in the right way.

Where?

Types of market

Having an understanding of the market will in many cases depend on the type of market that you are operating in.

Local businesses have a completely different view from *national* or *multinational* companies. A local curtain maker is not interested in the total UK market for curtains. It needs to know the local demand and how to access that demand.

All markets used to be *physical* – that is buyers and sellers meeting face to face such as in a shop. Today there is an increasing trend for *electronic or virtual* trading. High Street travel agents are struggling as more people book their holidays, flights and hotels over the internet. Firms who still have a strong High Street presence also offer goods by internet shopping.

There is also a distinction between *consumer markets* and *industrial markets*.

- Consumer markets sell to the end user – the general public.
- Industrial markets are when businesses sell to other businesses. Selling to industrial markets requires a slightly different approach. The relationship between the supplier and the customer will often be closer. In some cases the supplier will work with the customer to produce goods specifically for their business.

What?

Market knowledge should be easy for a small business with close day-to-day contact with its customers. However, knowledge is not the same as understanding. The owner needs to know how customers will react to changes in the product or prices. Selling to customers is an ever-changing activity; tastes change and so does the level of competition.

A new business will not have any market knowledge and should ensure that it understands the market before it starts trading.

The first thing a business needs to understand is the **demand** for its product or service.

Demand

Demand is when a customer wishes to buy a product. Effective demand is when a customer is able to buy the product, i.e. can afford it. There are several factors that determine the level of demand.

1 Price
- Higher priced goods will have lower demand as fewer people have the income to afford them. Very few people can afford a Porsche.
- The price of a competitor's product will influence demand for yours. Their price cut hits you rather than them.
- If the price is seen as *too* cheap it may limit the demand for goods based on prestige.

2 Income
- The general level of economic activity will determine the level of income. In a recession people will have less to spend and this will affect demand. When the economy grows, demand for goods and services will also rise.
- Individually, a higher income will mean more spending power. However this may cause a shift from cheaper goods to luxury goods.

3 Actions of competitors
In most cases there will be other firms offering the same or similar goods. If the consumer is able to shop around they will almost always opt for a cheaper product. The effect on demand will depend on:
- how similar the products are;
- how easy it is for consumers to make price comparisons.

4 Marketing
Both the firm's own marketing and that of its competitors will affect demand. A strong marketing campaign or a strong brand image can help increase demand even if the price is higher.

5 Seasonal factors
Demand for products may have distinct patterns. Not many garden chairs are sold in November. For a new garden centre, opened in March, it can be very difficult to judge sales and cash flows for the first winter.

The business also needs to have some idea of the *demand trends*. Is the market growing? If the market is declining it will be much harder for a new business to break into it.

How?

To be able to calculate demand the firm must break the market down. A good place to start is the size of the market. **Market size** can be measured by volume or value.

- Volume gives the quantity, which may be in units such as number of cars sold, by weight such as tonnes of wheat or by volume such as litres of petrol.
- Value is a measure of how much customers spend on the product. It will be quantity sold multiplied by the price per unit.

Without this information a firm cannot measure its share and its competitors' share of the sales.

The next step is to understand **market share**. Market share is the percentage of a market held by any one company or product. For many firms the main aim is to be the market leader, in other words to have the largest market share. For a new business it is important to understand the level of competition in the market. This will determine how easy it will be to break into the market. *Barriers to entry* are likely to be greater if one or several large firms dominate the market.

Another useful way of breaking down the market is **market segmentation**. This is dividing the market into smaller sections by customer characteristics. Adults and children or males and females. Another way is by age. It is generally accepted that elderly people have different buying patterns from teenagers.

For a new business estimating market share will be difficult and guesses may have to be made as to how much of the market they can hope to capture.

Exam insight

When analysing the market for a product or service take care to note if the figures are units or value. Depending on the nature of the business, it may be in more than one market and the way in which these markets behave may be very different.

Why?

Understanding the market is essential for all firms. Whatever industry or sector the firm operates in, it needs to know about its market. For a new business not understanding the market can lead to expensive mistakes. Having good market knowledge gives the firm the background in which to begin the process of selling to the customer.

Application

Dr Julie Diem Le worked as an eye sugeon for the NHS. She spotted a business idea whilst trying to buy sunglasses for her small niece. Although there were many sun protection products for children there was a definite gap in the market. After seeing the damage the sun could do she decided to set up her own business Zoobug – selling sunglasses for children. She used an Italian designer to design the glasses – they appeal to both children and parents but importantly protect from UV light. After a year she was selling 2000 pairs of sunglasses to upmarket opticians and Selfridges. Her sales were however lower than she had expected and she identified three reasons for this.

1 Poor weather in the UK.
2 The high price of the product.
3 The target customer age range was set too high.

This led her to develop a new plan for the future.

1 Start selling overseas.
2 Introduce optical frames as well as sunglasses.
3 Reduce price levels.
4 Adjust the age range to include younger children.

Understanding the market and developing a strategy to deal with it has helped the business to continue to expand. She is now selling in 20 countries.

Evaluation

There is little doubt that all firms need to understand their markets. Without this vital information any other marketing effort could be wasted. Understanding the market is perhaps the most important contribution that marketing makes to the profitability of the firm. The most important aspects of this process are to understand customer tastes, attitudes and behaviour.

Key Terms

Barriers to entry – factors that make it difficult for a new firm to enter a market

Brand image – a recognisable name or image that helps to support the product

Demand trends – the future pattern of demand

Industrial markets – businesses selling to other businesses

Target market – the group of or types of customer that the firm wants for its product or brand

Test yourself

1 How can firms measure the size of the market? (2)
2 Which market/s are the following in?
  Saga Holidays
  Top Shop
  British Gas (6)
3 Identify three factors that influence the level of demand. (3)
4 If total bicycle sales are 840,000 units and mountain bike sales are 21,000 units, what is the market share for mountain bikes? (2)
5 Identify two important things that a new business needs to know about its market and explain why these are important. (8)

Unit 8 · Sources of finance

What?

All businesses need money to start up, to operate and to expand. Where the money comes from is known as *sources of finance*.

Why?

Starting up

When a business starts out it needs money:

- to invest in long-term assets such as equipment and buildings. These require one-off spending, e.g. buying a 10-year lease on a shop;
- to purchase supplies, pay wages and to pay day-to-day bills such as water and electricity.

Growing

Once a business is established it will generate income from sales. This revenue will allow it to pay the bills and if the revenue is greater than the operating costs then it will have some *profit* remaining. This profit could be taken out of the business as *dividends* or kept in the business (*retained profit*). Initially it is wise to leave as much retained profit in the business as possible.

If the business wants to expand it may be able to do this by using the retained profit but it could need to find additional finance. The firm may also need additional finance if it runs into cash flow problems.

Where?

Finance for business comes either from the business itself (internal) or from outside the business (external).

Internal sources

- *Retained profit*: keeping profit in the business is known as retained profit. This provides over 60 per cent of the finance for the average business.
- *Cash flow management*: careful cash management, such as cutting back on stock levels and getting money in from customers sooner will help to stretch finance further.
- *Sale of assets*: selling assets that are no longer needed can release funding into the business.

External sources

If the business is unable to find sufficient funds internally then it may need to look to external sources. There are three major sources of external funding: loan capital, share capital and trade credit.

- *Loan capital*: this is borrowing. The most common source is from a bank usually for a fixed period of time. Short-term loans run for one or two years, medium-term from three to five years and long-term means more than five years. The bank will charge interest on the loan either at a fixed rate or at a rate that varies depending on the bank rate set by the Bank of England.

  A more flexible form of lending is an *overdraft*. This is a very short-term loan that allows the company to borrow what it needs (up to a preset limit) on a day-to-day basis. Bank overdrafts are the commonest form of borrowing for small businesses.

  Before lending, the bank will want to be sure that the firm will be able to meet the interest payments and repay the loan. Especially for a new business they will want some collateral (security) that may be a personal asset such as a house. During the 2008/09 'credit crunch', many small firms found out the disadvantage of flexible overdrafts; banks demanded their money back, forcing some firms into liquidation.

- *Share capital*: when a business starts up the owner often uses his own money. In the case of a Limited business this is known as share capital. If the business wishes to raise more external finance it can do this by selling shares to other people. In order to do this the business must be a limited company. This finance could come from individuals (private investors) or from other businesses such as *venture capital* firms. *Venture capitalists* invest in firms that they think have good prospects. They will want to have a part share in the business and often a management role. They are often prepared to invest in riskier businesses as they spread the risk over several businesses. Hopefully the highly successful ventures will more than compensate for the failures.

  Larger successful firms looking for greater levels of finance can sell shares to the public by becoming a plc (public limited company) and selling shares through the Stock Exchange. Smaller companies will normally be limited to the Alternative Investment Market (AIM).

- *Trade credit*: this is the simplest form of external finance. The business gets goods or services from others but does not pay for them immediately. The average credit period is two months. This means that the business has use of the funds until it has to make the payment. New small firms are unlikely to get trade credit until they have been established for a few years.

How much?

How much finance is available will depend on several factors. These are:

- The type of business – sole traders will be limited to the owner's own funds and any loans that may be available. A private limited company can raise capital by selling shares to friends and family. A plc will be able to sell shares directly to the public.
- The stage of development of the business – new businesses will find it much harder to raise finance than established firms.
- How successful the firm is – a successful track record will encourage lenders and investors.
- The state of the economy – when the economy is growing, lenders and investors are confident about the future. Interest rates also affect the amount of funding that is available. Higher interest rates make borrowing more expensive.

Finance should be *adequate and appropriate*. Start-ups require good planning and adequate financing.

- **Adequate financing** means that there must be sufficient funding. This is not just for the new machinery or buildings but also the working capital requirements to pay staff and buy raw materials. New business start-ups often underestimate the amount of cash that they will need and running out of cash is a major reason for new business failure.
- **Appropriate financing** means that the funding should suit the project. The purchase of a fixed asset needs long-term financing. A short-term cash requirement requires a short-term financing solution.

Application

Robert Wiseman started out as a milkman and now his business is the UK's third largest milk producer. In 1985 Wiseman and his two brothers used their houses as security to raise enough funds to buy a dairy. This had five milk rounds and eight employees. Instead of supplying households the business concentrated on supplying shops. This strategy was very successful and enabled the business to grow significantly. However in 1994 they realised that they could not continue to finance expansion from cash flow. They decided to float the company on the stock market, selling 25 per cent of the business to raise £14 million. With this funding they bought other Scottish businesses and built a dairy in Manchester and Droitwich. Now the business has annual revenues of around £390 million and employs more than 3,000 people.

This successful business started with the usual difficulty faced by new businesses of how to secure funding. In this case the owners offered their homes as security so were able to obtain a bank loan, they reinvested profits and the stock exchange float enabled them to raise additional funding to continue to develop the business.

Evaluation

A new business will inevitably find raising finance to be one of the most difficult aspects of starting the business. Lack of adequate funding is one of the major causes of business failure. This raises a huge dilemma for lenders. They need to be cautious about lending but also need to take some chances. The 'credit crunch' of 2008 has brought these dilemmas into clear focus.

Key Terms

Capital expenditure – spending by the business on fixed assets

Overtrading – when a firm expands without adequate or appropriate funding

Plc – public limited company; a business with limited liability whose shares can be advertised for sale on the stock exchange

Test yourself

1. What is meant by capital expenditure? (2)
2. List two internal sources of finance. (2)
3. Explain two types of business finance provided by banks. (4)
4. What is trade credit? List one disadvantage of using this method of funding. (4)
5. Explain why a new firm might find it difficult to get external finance. (4)
6. Outline two sources of finance suitable for long-term development. (4)

Unit 9 Location factors for business start-ups

What?

Location decisions are always difficult and always important. For a service business such as a restaurant, location may be the single most important factor. The entrepreneur must weigh up the high cost of a top location with the lower rent on a poorer location. Within the same city, a top location may cost 10 times as much as a poorer one.

The table below explains the main factors a business start-up should consider when choosing a location and indicates which types of business will find some factors more important than others.

Factor	Explanation	Especially relevant for	Less important for
Cost of land	More attractive, larger sites cost more, meaning there is less capital left for covering other costs	Start-ups needing a busy location, often in town or city centres – often service or retail businesses such as restaurants	Manufacturing or internet based start-ups can look for sites with low-cost land
Space	More space costs more money; some firms need plenty of storage space; others need space for possible future expansion	Those selling bulky products, often manufacturers and those who need to hold large stocks	Those needing prime sites for whom the cost of large space will be prohibitive
Accessibility of suppliers	All firms need supplies of either materials or products for resale; suppliers should be able to reach the business quickly and easily	Firms needing daily deliveries and those where supplies are bulky but finished product may be easier to transport	Those for whom nearness to the market is of greater importance
Labour	If skilled staff are to be recruited the business location must be close enough to well populated areas	Firms that rely heavily on skilled staff, especially if those skills tend to be concentrated regionally, e.g. financial trading in the City of London	Businesses that use a lot of machinery or equipment instead of using people
Market	The proximity of large numbers of potential customers	Service suppliers such as nail bars or barbers need customers to be able to visit them regularly – so must be close to customers	Service sector firms that sell mostly via the internet or are manufacturers have little need to be close to their customers
Infrastructure	Services, such as transport links, telecommunications services. Health and education services are referred to together as **infrastructure**	Telecoms services are likely to be important to any online business, and almost every business needs well-developed transport infrastructure	Due to the nature of their business, primary sector firms, such as farms, will often be located in areas with relatively less developed local services
Government intervention	In a few parts of the country, such as Northern Ireland or the North East, government **grants** might be available for new businesses	Start-ups that will create jobs for the unemployed, and those starting up in economically deprived areas	Government assistance is available in very few areas, and few businesses in those areas are eligible

How?

For a high street service business such as a clothes shop or a café, the success of a location will boil down to five main factors:

- the numbers of pedestrians walking by;
- the amount of car traffic;
- the ease of parking nearby;
- how well the locality fits the image of the new business;
- the cost of the premises.

An intelligent way of choosing a location is to shortlist two or three promising sites. Then to use a grid such as the following to help make a decision. In this case the higher the number the better.

Example: for choosing the location for a hairdressers

Category	Mark range	Location A	Location B
1. Number of pedestrians walking by	1–10	8	4
2. Amount of car traffic	1–5	5	2
3. Ease of parking nearby	1–5	1	4
4. How well locality fits the image	1–20	15	8
5. The cost of premises	1–10	1*	8
TOTAL	5–50	30	26

*1 = very expensive

Clearly, if the business was a pound shop, you would change the mark ranges. Image would be much less important, and the cost of premises much more important.

Exam insight

How to make your judgement

Since most location questions will ask you to suggest which factors are important for the business discussed in the exam paper, application marks will rely on selecting which location factors are important for the firm described. Crucial questions to ask are: do customers need to visit? How reliant is the firm on regular deliveries of bulky supplies? How tight is cash flow for the start-up? The table above should help you to distinguish which factors are most important using your answers to these questions.

Key Terms

Grants – the offer of cash to part-fund a business cost such as machinery; such grants are sometimes available from government, and (for under-25s) may be available from the Prince's Trust

Infrastructure – the provision of the basics needed for life, e.g. water, electricity and transport such as roads and railways

Themes for evaluation

Good locations cost. Better locations are likely to be in greater demand and therefore the cost of those locations will always be high. Since many business start-ups seem constantly short of cash, they are frequently forced into selecting non-prime locations, maybe just off the High Street, or tucked away down a country lane. Money saved with a cheaper location means more cash available for other aspects of the business such as marketing. However, it is often worth asking whether these savings are often at the heart of any problems the business is experiencing. Unreliable deliveries from suppliers may be the result of a tucked away location. The most common problem, though, is that cheap locations have little passing trade, meaning it is hard to grab potential customers' attention in the first place.

Test yourself

1. Outline two reasons why a business start-up may choose a location which it knows is hard to reach for customers. (4)
2. Explain why a specialist model-making shop is more likely to survive in a small parade of shops away from the city centre than a burger bar. (6)
3. Outline two reasons why the availability of labour may be a crucial factor in a location decision. (4)
4. For each of the following firms, state and briefly justify, which is the most important location factor:
   a) a small bottler of fresh apple juice
   b) a small web design business specialising in complex website design for the financial services industry
   c) a cheap fashion jeweller's shop. (6)

Unit 10 Employing people

What?

There are two situations in which business start-ups may need to employ staff. The first – and most difficult – is hiring staff in advance of the actual start date. Examples include opening a restaurant or starting up a motorbike delivery service. Hiring in advance of start-up has huge implications – especially for pressures on the firm's cash flow. (Imagine having to hire and pay twelve restaurant staff for two weeks' training before a penny has come in from customers.)

The second requirement for staff will be much easier to cope with. The business may have been opened by one person, but be doing so well that staff are quickly required. In this case there is a far better chance that cash inflows from the successful business will help to finance the new salary bills.

Recruiting staff to work for the business might offer overworked entrepreneurs a number of benefits:
- reduced hours;
- reduced stress levels leading to better decision-making;
- the opportunity to bring in people to help with specific skills the entrepreneur lacks, such as bookkeeping.

Unfortunately, if you ask people running smallish businesses about their biggest headache, the majority will answer 'staff'. Recruiting, training and managing staff requires a set of skills that many entrepreneurs lack.

Taking on staff can also be daunting due to the legal responsibilities involved in employing people. This adds an extra burden to an entrepreneur who may already be overstretched. Before employing staff, entrepreneurs will need to research legal issues such as minimum wage, registering with the tax office and how to draw up contracts of employment.

How?

Deciding what recruitment is necessary should be based on the following two basic questions:
- What skills does the business need from an employee?
- How much time does the business need the employee to work?

Skills

Taking on an employee could give an entrepreneur the opportunity to employ somebody with a useful skill they themselves may lack. This could be a specialist business skill, such as a flair for marketing, or alternatively a skill related to the type of business, such as a restaurant employing a fully trained chef. Taking these opportunities could improve efficiency since qualified staff should be able to do a better job faster. Before deciding what recruitment is necessary, the entrepreneur should analyse which skills the business is lacking.

Time

When employing people, businesses face two fundamental choices:
- temporary or permanent;
- full-time or part-time.

Permanent staff are employed with a legal contract without an end date. Temporary staff on the other hand will be employed for a limited period of time, at the end of which they will cease working for the business unless another contract is offered by the business.

Temporary staff		Permanent staff	
Advantages to the business	Disadvantages to the business	Advantages to the business	Disadvantages to the business
A more flexible way of employing staff, since it is relatively easy to adjust staffing levels if sales decline	Employees may lack motivation as they feel little loyalty or commitment to the business	Should be more committed to the business	Harder to get rid of if the business decides the member of staff is no longer needed
A simple way to gain expertise the firm lacks, such as an IT specialist to create an online booking system	Can be hard to build a sense of team spirit if individuals never stay for long	Makes investment in training more worthwhile as permanent staff will stay with the business longer	Business may get stale if the supply of new ideas from outside dries up

Staff are generally considered part-time if they are employed for less than 30 hours per week on average. You or your friends may have direct experience of part-time work, making it easier to consider the pros and cons of part-timers from the point of view of an employer.

Full-time		Part-time	
Advantages to the business	Disadvantages to the business	Advantages to the business	Disadvantages to the business
Staff always around for meetings	Less flexible than using part-time staff	May be more flexible when asked to cover for absent colleagues	May be hard to arrange meetings for all staff
May be more likely to be committed to the business than part-timers	Full-timers can become complacent, believing the job is theirs by right	May be on **zero-hours contracts**, allowing employers to offer no hours work in a slow week	Other priorities may lead to less commitment to the business

Using consultants and advisors

Getting 'experts' into the business to help out on a short-term basis may allow an entrepreneur to access skills they lack themselves or within their workforce. A good example is hiring a consultant to build a lively, e-commerce-enabled website. Jamie Oliver might be able to set up a good restaurant, but why should he have web skills?

All too often, however, the use of a **business consultant** or advisor can leave plenty of negative effects without finding a solution to the problem, such as:

- high cost of using consultants;
- failure to fully understand a business they are only working with for a short spell;
- tendency to offer short-term, quick-fix solutions rather than finding the underlying causes of problems;
- tendency to do what they think is wanted by the manager who hired them ('doing their dirty work' for them).

Key Terms

Business consultant – an individual with specific expertise hired to complete a specific task
Zero-hours contracts – a contract of employment that promises nothing to the employee, but enables the employer to get the employee to work when needed

Exam insight

If asked to recommend whether a business should employ part-time or full-time staff or permanent or temporary staff, the crucial deciding factor will be the level of flexibility the business is likely to need. Both part-timers and temporary contracts tend to offer greater flexibility to the employer (perhaps at the cost of the employees' rights). Judgement is required on whether the firm is likely to face stable or erratic demand. In obvious cases such as running an ice cream parlour, temporary or part-time staff will usually be a better option.

Themes for evaluation

Though rarely recognised in textbooks, and similarly rarely explored in exams, a significant proportion of 'employing people' in small businesses occurs unofficially. Many shops are staffed entirely by family members, who may or may not receive a wage for their work. And some people are hired on a casual, 'cash in hand' basis, with no notification given to tax authorities. Such practices seem relatively harmless, but if the term 'child labour' was used, it would seem like exploitation. Similarly, casual employment can mean a casual approach to issues such as health and safety. Though entrepreneurs often find the legislation governing employing staff a burden and complain of too much 'red tape', those working for any business need some kind of protection by the law. The real debate is whether the right balance has been struck between the interests of employees and those of the employers.

Test yourself

1. Identify two legal issues an entrepreneur must consider when employing people for the first time. (2)
2. Distinguish between part-time and temporary staff. (3)
3. For each of the following small businesses, state and explain whether they are likely to be better off employing permanent or temporary staff:
   a) a fruit grower
   b) an IT troubleshooter who'll visit your house to fix your PC
   c) a firm manufacturing novelty gifts for the London Olympics. (9)
4. Analyse one benefit and one drawback of schools using contracted staff to run their canteens. (6)

3 Financial planning

Unit 11 Calculating revenue, costs and profit

What?

Business revenue

Revenue is the income a firm receives from selling the product or service that it provides. The total revenue for a firm for any given period can be calculated by multiplying the selling price (revenue per unit) by the number of units sold in that period.

Exam insight

A surprising number of students muddle revenue with profit. They think that revenue means 'you're making a lot of money'. But if the high revenues are matched by high costs, you're not making a penny. The 'Dragons' often use a well-known business phrase: 'Revenue is vanity; profit is sanity'.

Costs

Accountants classify costs in several ways. For now, the important distinction to make is what happens to costs when the firm's output changes.

- *Variable costs* – a variable cost is one that varies in direct proportion to output. In other words, if a firm makes twice as many bags of crisps, they will need twice as many potatoes. Variable costs are often expressed per unit produced, i.e. variable cost per unit. They can also be given as the total variable costs: variable cost per unit x quantity produced.
- *Fixed costs* – a fixed cost is one that does not change in relation to output. An example might be managers' salaries – they remain the same whether 10,000 or 20,000 bags of crisps are produced per month.
- *Total costs* – this is the figure gained by adding the total variable costs at any level of output to the fixed costs being paid by the business.

Profit

Profit is the excess of revenue over costs. In terms of a formula, this can be expressed as:

$$\text{profit} = \text{total revenue} - \text{total costs}$$

This equation can be broken down as follows:

$$\text{profit} = (\text{quantity sold} \times \text{selling price}) - [(\text{quantity sold} \times \text{variable cost per unit}) + \text{fixed costs}]$$

Why?

The quest for profit lies at the heart of the objectives of almost every business. Questioning in exams is likely to focus upon the ways to boost profit. The analytical approach to any question on profit is to consider how profit is calculated and work through each part of the profit equation.

Total revenue (selling price x quantity sold)

Increasing total revenue will boost profit unless costs rise faster. To increase revenue, one of two variables must increase:

- *Selling price* – price can be increased, but, for most products, an increase in price will lead to a fall in quantity sold. Therefore, any decision on whether price would increase profit must be linked to the concept of price elasticity of demand (see Unit 44) – the responsiveness of demand to a change in price.
- *Number of units sold* – a firm trying to increase its profit may seek to boost the number of units sold, perhaps by promoting the product or changing the product in some way. Successfully increasing the quantity sold will increase the total variable costs. It may also go hand in hand with a change in some other part of the profit equation – perhaps the increase in sales was the result of an advertising campaign (increased fixed costs), or better quality materials (increased variable costs per unit). Another way of increasing the quantity sold is to reduce the selling price – but will this lead to an increase or decrease in total revenue? Only price elasticity has the answer to this question.

Total costs

Any action that successfully reduces total costs without hitting revenue will increase profit. However, you should always remember that no business will be deliberately ignoring easy cost-cutting measures

– answers that suggest that cost cutting carries no further implications are simplistic and will not impress examiners.

Variable costs

Materials and components are the most obvious variable costs faced by firms. In order to reduce the variable cost per unit, you might suggest that the firm could use lower quality and therefore cheaper materials. However, a dip in the quality of the product might affect sales in the medium to long term. Therefore total revenue could fall in line with variable costs. Alternatively, a suggestion that buying materials in greater bulk would allow the firm to experience bulk-buying discounts should be qualified by an awareness that this may lead to increased stock-holding costs (usually fixed costs).

Fixed costs

A reduction in fixed costs is another route to greater profit. However, moving to a factory with cheaper rent may create very significant short-term relocation costs along with a probable halt to production while the move occurred. Cutting staff salaries would also reduce fixed costs but would do little to enhance staff morale and may therefore lead to less efficient production.

How?

The answer is likely to lie in the question. Read the stimulus material carefully in order to try to identify whether there are any potential cost savings that may be appropriate. Alternatively, increased profit may be achievable by boosting revenue in some way that avoids increasing costs significantly.

Key Terms

Fixed cost – a cost that does not change in relation to output
Profit – the surplus of revenue over total costs; if total costs exceed revenue the firm has made a loss
Variable cost – a cost that varies in direct proportion to output

Exam insight

When proposing how to boost profit, keep thinking about timescale. Is the firm pursuing short- or long-term objectives? To increase short-term profit, higher prices and lower cost/quality materials may work well – but both approaches may damage long-term profitability.

Application

Boosting profit in a favourable external environment	Boosting profit when the external environment is against a firm
In good trading periods, profit boosts are likely to stem from increases in revenue. These may be the result of increased sales volumes or the ability to increase selling price without significantly reducing sales.	If the external environment is unfavourable, a company will be very unlikely to be able to boost its revenues. Any increases in profit are likely to stem from cost reductions. However, it is important to consider the implications of any cost cutting, for example the effect on staff morale of laying off workers or the effect on the firm's image of using cheaper raw materials.

What next?

There are two ways that a firm can choose to use its profit:

- retain the profit in the business and use it to buy extra assets that will help the firm in the future – perhaps extra machinery or equipment that will allow them to grow;
- pay out profit to the owners of the business. In some cases this will be necessary in order to keep the owners happy and avoid them withdrawing their investment.

The majority of businesses will actually choose to split their profit between these two uses, varying the proportion to each use depending upon their current circumstances and especially their need for extra finance.

Test yourself

1 Identify two variable and two fixed costs of running a car wash. (4)
2 Firm X has variable costs per unit of £5. Revenue is £12,000 earned by selling 1,000 units. If they made £2,000 profit, what are their fixed costs? (4)
3 Firm Y makes a profit of £5,000 by selling 1,000 units for £10 each. If fixed costs are £3,000, what are the variable costs per unit? (4)
4 SofaCo is a manufacturer of sofas.
   a) Outline one action it could take concerning its variable costs to try to increase profit. (2)
   b) Explain why that action might cause long-term problems for the business. (6)

Unit 12 Break-even analysis

AQA Business Studies for AS Revision Guide

What?

Break-even is the term used to describe a situation in which a firm is making neither a profit nor a loss. In other words, it is generating enough revenue to cover its costs, but no more. Break-even occurs at a level of output where total revenue and total costs are equal. A firm's break-even point is frequently shown on a break-even chart. This is a diagram that shows the firm's fixed costs, total costs and total revenue at all possible levels of output. The break-even point occurs where the total revenue and total cost lines meet.

How?

In order to construct a break-even chart, it is best to draw up a table showing costs and revenues at three different levels of sales, usually where output is zero, at maximum output and at an easy figure in between. Take this example:

- Selling price = £10
- Variable costs per unit = £5
- Fixed costs = £1,000 per month
- Maximum output = 250 units per month

OUTPUT	0	100	250
Variable costs	£0	£500	£1,250
Fixed costs	£1,000	£1,000	£1,000
Total costs	£1,000	£1,500	£2,250
Total revenue	£0	£1,000	£2,500

With the table drawn up, the fixed and total cost and total revenue lines can be plotted on a graph, showing output on the horizontal axis and £s on the vertical.

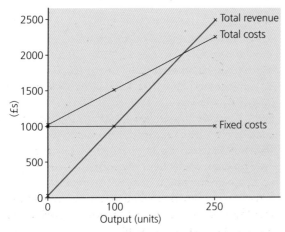

Fig. 12A: Break-even chart

Why?

Identify profit/loss at any level of output

The chart makes it possible to see profit or loss at any given level of output. Look along the horizontal axis to the output level that is being considered, then read upwards and measure the vertical gap between the total revenue and total cost lines. That gap represents the profit (if revenue is higher) or loss (if costs are higher than revenue). Figure 12A shows a loss of £500 if only 100 units are sold.

Identify safety margin

Safety margin is the term given to the difference between the current level of sales and the break-even output. On the break-even chart, the safety margin is the horizontal distance from current sales to the break-even point, as shown:

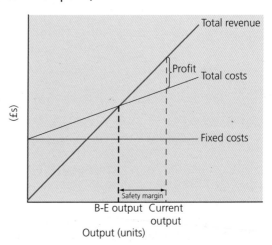

Fig. 12B: Break-even chart 2

How (without the graph)?

The break-even output of a firm can be calculated, without the need to draw a graph. The calculation required is shown below:

$$\text{Break-even point} = \frac{\text{Fixed costs}}{\text{selling price} - \text{variable costs per unit}}$$

For example, the firm whose figures are shown above would have a break-even output of:

$$\frac{£1,000}{£10 - £5} = 200 \text{ units}$$

When?

Break-even analysis is always a useful tool, for both large and small firms. In effect, the banks that collapsed in the 2008/09 credit crunch had failed to consider their own safety margin. The type of business that will make the most use of break-even analysis includes:

1 Entrepreneurs opening their first outlet, who need to estimate whether they can get enough customers to cover all the costs. So break-even analysis forms a key part of most **business plans**.

2 A small firm facing a difficult period such as a recession and needs to estimate whether it will manage to avoid losses in the future.

3 Any business with a single product line (for example, Domino's Pizza) that needs to make a decision, such as, 'Should we put the price up by £1' or 'Should we double the amount we spend on advertising?' Adjusting the lines on a break-even chart gives an answer to questions like these.

Pros and cons of break-even analysis

'What if?' questions can be asked – the technique allows firms to see what would happen to costs and revenues if variables, such as selling price, or capacity, were changed by a simple adjustment to the break-even chart. The technique provides a graphical focus of attention for meetings.

But

Break-even is based on two key assumptions:

1 That the firm sells every unit it makes – in other words the firm is not manufacturing for stock.

2 That all the lines on the chart are assumed to be straight (linearity). This means that variable costs are the same for every unit manufactured, and every unit is sold for the same price. This is often far from the real situation, with some products sold at a discount and some firms able to bulk buy cheaper materials after reaching a certain level of output.

Application

Who does it work for?

Break-even is particularly useful for firms that:	Break-even is of limited use to firms that:
Make and sell one standard product	Are subject to severe seasonality

Break-even is particularly useful for firms that:	Break-even is of limited use to firms that:
Only make products to order – meaning all output is sold	Find it hard to identify the actual variable and fixed costs involved in making their product
Only operate in one market	Operate in fast-moving markets

Themes for evaluation

Quality of information used

Any decision-making technique is only as good as the information used in its construction. Break-even charts will be of limited use if selling prices and cost levels are being roughly estimated, for example in a business start-up.

Validity beyond the very near future?

Break-even is a technique used to try to assess the firm's future position. Many firms will be able to calculate how many units they must sell next week in order to break-even, but few will be in a stable enough environment to work out an annual break-even output.

Test yourself

1 a) Calculate the number of units that would need to be sold to break-even if a firm sells its products for £5 per unit, has variable costs of £2 per unit and fixed costs of £6,000. (2)

b) If the firm is currently selling 2,500 units, what is its safety margin? (2)

2 Briefly explain three key benefits of carrying out break-even analysis for a toilet paper manufacturer. (6)

3 Outline three problems that may be experienced by a computer manufacturer using break-even analysis to plan for the next year. (6)

4 Which key variables would a leisure centre need to identify in order to use break-even analysis? Use examples in your answers. (4)

Unit 13 Cash flow management and forecasting

What?

Cash flow is the flow of money into and out of the business in a given period of time. Cash flow is not the same as profit. Profit is what is left for the business owners after all costs of operating have been deducted from revenue. Firms can be cash rich but unprofitable or profitable but have cash flow problems.

Why?

Cash flow is vital. It is essential that bills are paid when they come due. Suppliers will refuse to continue supplying raw materials if they are not paid. In extreme cases creditors may take the firm to court, which could result in the company being put into liquidation.

Cash flow problems are the most common reason for business failure. Cash flow forecasting attempts to predict the future flow of cash into and out of the business. Doing this means that the business can take measures to ensure that enough cash is available when it is needed.

Who?

All businesses need to monitor their cash position.

It is particularly important that new firms have sufficient funding if they are going to survive. It is estimated that 70 per cent of new businesses fail in their first year because of cash flow problems. However, larger established firms can also face cash flow problems. General Motors and Newcastle Football Club both faced cash flow problems recently.

When a firm wants to borrow money, the bank will almost certainly want to see a cash flow forecast. They do this to ensure that the business has enough cash to enable it to survive. They also want to be sure that the business will be able to repay the loan and to make the interest payments.

When?

Businesses need to manage cash flow by continually reviewing their present and future cash position. This allows the firm to:
● anticipate the timing and seriousness of any cash shortage;
● arrange financial cover for the shortfall period;
● review timings of cash received and paid out.

How?

Preparing a cash flow forecast

To prepare a cash flow forecast businesses need to work out what will happen financially in the business. All money coming into and out of the business needs to be estimated.

These flows of money are then set on to a grid showing the cash movements in each month.

Cash inflow

In this example the business is a new start-up – a restaurant. The business will receive an injection of capital of £20,000. This will be received in January and is shown as income.

The restaurant will open in February and expects a slow start with sales gradually building each month.

It is important that the revenue from sales is shown when the cash is received not when the sale is made.

	January	February	March	April	May
Income					
Capital	20,000				
Sales		2,000	4,000	4,500	6,000
Total income	**20,000**	**2,000**	**4,000**	**4,500**	**6,000**

Cash outflow

● In January the restaurant will buy furniture and kitchen equipment costing £17,000.
● Ingredients will cost £800 in the first month increasing as sales increase.
● Rent for the building costs £1,000 per month but the owner requires two months' rent in advance.
● Wages are estimated to be £1,500 per month and there are other expenses of £400 per month.

When these figures have been entered on to the grid the total expenditure can be calculated.

Expenditure	January	February	March	April	May
Equipment	17,000				
Materials	0	800	900	1,000	1,200
Rent	2,000	1,000	1,000	1,000	1,000
Wages		1,500	1,500	1,500	1,500
Other expenses		400	400	400	400
Total expenditure	**19,000**	**3,700**	**3,800**	**3,900**	**4,100**

The cash flow forecast can now be completed by calculating:

● **Monthly balance**

This is revenue for the month minus expenditure for the month. It shows each month if there is more income than expenditure. In this case income is greater than revenue except in February. When expenditure is greater than revenue the monthly balance will be negative. This is shown in brackets to indicate that it is a minus figure.

● **Opening and closing balance**

This is rather like a mini bank statement. It shows what cash the business has at the beginning of the month (opening balance) and what the cash position is at the end of the month (closing balance). The closing balance is the opening balance plus the monthly balance. Take care with negative balances!

The closing balance shows the business the net cash position each month.

The completed cash flow forecast will be:

	January	February	March	April	May
Income					
Capital	20,000				
Sales		2,000	4,000	4,500	6,000
Total income	**20,000**	**2,000**	**4,000**	**4,500**	**6,000**
Expenditure					
Equipment	17,000				
Materials	0	800	900	1,000	1,200
Rent	2,000	1,000	1,000	1,000	1,000
Wages		1,500	1,500	1,500	1,500
Other expenses		400	400	400	400
Total expenditure	**19,000**	**3,700**	**3,800**	**3,900**	**4,100**
Monthly balance	1,000	(1,700)	200	600	1,900
Opening balance	0	1000	(700)	(500)	100
Closing balance	**1,000**	**(700)**	**(500)**	**100**	**2,000**

What does it show?

The cash flow forecast shows that there is a negative cash balance for the months of February and March. Only in April does the business start having a positive cash flow. As there is no such thing as negative money this cash flow forecast shows the business that it must take action if it is to avoid problems in the early months. It needs to borrow an extra £700 or delay some outgoings.

But

The usefulness of cash flow forecasts depends on how well prepared the estimates are. A cash flow forecast can alert the business to possible future cash problems. It cannot take into account unforeseen circumstances that might affect the business. When a new business is starting up it can help to ensure that the venture does not fail for lack of adequate funding. This will depend on sales and costs forecasts actually being realistic.

Key Terms

Creditors – individuals or other businesses that are owed money by the business

Debtors – individuals or companies that owe money to the business

Liabilities – what the business owes

Liquidation – being forced to hand your business over to a liquidator, who will sell off the firm's assets to repay its debts; this usually means the business closes down

Exam insight

When constructing a cash flow forecast, remember to show cash in and out when it is actually received or paid.

When suggesting how a firm can improve its cash flow position, look at what is realistic for the firm. A small firm is unlikely to be able to demand early payment from its customers.

Themes for evaluation

There is little doubt that cash flow management is important for businesses, especially new start-ups, which are more likely to face cash flow problems. Cash flow forecasting is also useful for existing businesses when they are looking at expansion or taking on additional business. However, cash flow forecasts are only a tool to assist managers. They do not ensure business survival. Managers need to be aware of any changes in the economic and market climate that they are operating in – and change their plans and strategies accordingly.

Test yourself

1 What is meant by cash flow? (2)
2 What is a cash flow forecast? (2)
3 Why is having sufficient cash important for the business? (4)
4 Which is more important: cash flow or profit? (4)
5 Give two reasons why a bank might want to see a cash flow forecast before giving the business a loan. (2)
6 Outline two possible solutions to a cash flow crisis caused by a short-term dip in sales for a crisp manufacturer. (4)
7 Fill in the blanks on the following cash flow forecast: (10)

	January	February	March	April
Cash in	100	110	120	120
Cash out	90	110	130	
Net cash flow		0		20
Opening balance	10			
Closing balance				

Unit 14 Setting budgets

What?

A budget is a target for costs or revenue that a firm or department must aim to reach over a given period of time. Examples of budgets include:

- Arsene Wenger being given a summer budget of £25 million to buy new players (and underspending it).
- The Secretary of State for Education being given a 2009/10 budget of £80,000 million to run all the schools and colleges in England and Wales.
- A manager of a small Tesco Express store being given a budget of £5,000 for recruitment advertising for the coming year.

Three budgets

Three sets of financial targets will usually be set within a business. These cover income, expenditure and profit. The income budget (Table 14A) shows how many units of a product should be sold and at what price. For a shop, this could translate to how many customers buy and what is their average spend. Multiplying these together gives a figure for total income for each period.

Table 14A The income budget

	Week 1	Week 2	Week 3	Week 4
Products sold	25	30	30	40
Average price	£10	£10	£12	£12
Income	£250	£300	£360	£480

An expenditure budget (Table 14B) will show planned spending on the typical costs for the business:

Table 14B The expenditure budget

	Week 1	Week 2	Week 3	Week 4
	£	£	£	£
Materials	120	150	150	200
Wages	100	100	100	100
Rent	100	100	100	100
Bills	40	40	40	40
Total expenditure	360	390	390	440

Finally, the bottom row of the income and expenditure budgets is combined to help form the profit budget:

Table 14C The profit budget

	Week 1	Week 2	Week 3	Week 4
	£	£	£	£
Income	250	300	360	480
Total expenditure	360	390	390	440
Profit	−110	−90	−30	40

Why are budgets needed?

Budgets are needed as a control tool once an organisation has grown to a size that prohibits the boss from making all spending decisions. Only the smallest organisations can operate without some kind of delegated spending power. In reality, most firms will need to have a system of budgets in place to allow those on the spot to decide where and when money needs to be spent, without the need to check with those in higher authority. A budget allows individuals or sections of the firm to be allocated a certain amount of money that they are permitted to spend. This frees up time for those who no longer need to sign off this expenditure.

How are they used?

- *As a control tool* – the allocation of sums that departments or individuals can spend allows spending to be constrained, ensuring that no area of the firm is running up costs that had not been planned for.
- *As a yardstick against which performance can be measured* – successful departments will exceed budgeted figures for revenues and keep costs below budgeted figures. In either case, the success of the budget holder can be easily measured and therefore recognised.

How are budgets set?

- *Incremental budgeting* – adding a certain percentage on to last year's budget to allow for inflation.
- *Zero budgeting* – setting each budget to zero at the start of each year and asking each budget holder

to justify every penny that is allocated to their budget. This is a time consuming and expensive process to go through each year but will ensure that budgets do not grow automatically.

Exam insight

It is important to distinguish between a forecast (what you expect to happen) and a budget. A budget is a target. Managers will be praised or criticised (or even sacked) depending on whether they beat or are beaten by their budgets.

Benefits of using a budgeting system

Budgets allow managers to practise what is known as management by exception. This is where they focus their attention on areas whose budgets show a large variance. This allows managers' time to be used more productively than if they were required to check every department's spending on a regular basis.

Delegating spending power to managers of separate departments may well have a motivational effect on the budget holders. Being trusted with the authority to decide how money should be spent may provide an increased feeling of responsibility.

Budgets in small business start-ups

The main reason for setting budgets when starting up a small business is to ensure that the entrepreneur has figures to aim for. Income budgets will be helpful in judging whether or not the business is selling enough at a good enough price to cover budgeted costs. Cost budgets can be used to provide a monitoring tool to check spending in the early months and years of the business.

The biggest problem in setting budgets for a start-up is that there are usually no past figures to use as a basis for income and expenditure estimates.

Key Terms

Budgeted profit – the minimum level of profit expected from a section of the business over a year.
Expenditure budget – the maximum spending allowed by a manager or department in the course of a year
Income budget – the minimum level of sales (by value) expected over a period of time.

Themes for evaluation

There is a danger that entrepreneurs might spend so much time on their budgets that they forget to run their actual business. Having plans is undoubtedly helpful, but accepting they will never be completely accurate is a necessary skill for an entrepreneur whose budgets will have been set based on a 'best guess'. Failure to reach income or profit targets or exceeding expenditure targets should stimulate an entrepreneur to ask, 'Why did it happen?' However, in many cases, certainly at the start of a business, the real answer will be that the targets set were unrealistic and need to be adjusted in the future.

Test yourself

1 Explain the meaning of the term 'management by exception'. (3)
2 Explain two benefits of introducing a system of budgeting for a rapidly growing small firm. (4)
3 Outline two problems that may result from using budgets as a strict tool for controlling costs. (4)
4 Briefly explain why accurate budgeting may be much harder for a manufacturer of high fashion clothing than a producer of washing machines. (5)
5 Explain two things that an entrepreneur may use to come up with figures when setting budgets for a brand new business start-up. (4)

 **Unit 15 Assessing business start-ups**

What?

Assessing means making a judgement based on weighing up arguments for and against. Therefore, assessing a business start-up means considering the strengths and weaknesses of the business plan.

Who?

The entrepreneur is, of course, constantly making judgements within every stage of the start-up. 'Assessing business start-ups' is a phrase that usually refers to others who need to appraise the business plan. This would include all those who may gain or lose financially from the new business such as bankers, partners and venture capital investors.

How?

The two main areas for assessment will be:
● objectives;
● strengths and weaknesses of the plan/idea.
Objectives (targets) for business start-ups are likely to fall into one of three categories:

Categories of start-up objectives and some typical examples:

Financial	Personal	Social
Break even within a year	Be my own boss	Keep local teenagers off the streets
Achieve sales of £20,000 per month by Christmas	Show what I can do	Send clothing to less developed countries
Make a profit of £10,000 in the first six months	Get out of my current job	Provide fresh water in less developed countries
Make enough from the business to pay myself a salary of £25,000 per year	Build something to pass on to my family	Be carbon neutral

Once the business has started trading, its success can be judged by monitoring whether it achieved its objectives. This is one of the reasons why good objectives should be precise and timed – allowing a judgement on whether success has been achieved.

Strengths and weaknesses of business ideas

A business idea, or model, should be easily summed up in just a few lines explaining what the business will actually do. Great business models can be the key to huge entrepreneurial success – such as easyJet's low cost air travel. Not all business models will be so spectacularly successful, but they will still offer one or more key strengths:
● a clear idea of how the business will meet an obvious need;
● a clear ability to meet the need at a cost that allows a profit to be made;
● potential for growth of the business to a level that will justify investor's risk-taking.

Among many brilliant business models have been:
● Innocent Drinks: blend fruit into convenient, healthy, pricey drinks
● Scoop Ice Cream: bring authentic, freshly made Italian ice cream to Britain's high streets
● Facebook: make a college-based social networking site available to everyone

Once entrepreneurs are clear on what the idea actually is, most will devise a business plan. This is the document that details exactly what is needed in order to start-up and run the business. Thorough business plans need not be long, but they should cover all major aspects for which a business needs to plan:
● clear objectives;
● clear staffing plan to include recruitment and selection;
● clear evidence of well-researched decisions on what suppliers to use;
● effective market research findings analysed and used to form a sensible, cost-effective marketing strategy;
● realistic financial forecasts of costs, revenues and therefore profits, showing the effect on profit of revenue or cost estimates being inaccurate.

A business plan that lacks these main features is likely to be judged inadequate by those who need to assess the start-up. In addition, judgements need to be made on the wisdom of the proposals, for example does it make sense to use a local supplier that is 40 per cent more expensive than supply prices from the Far East?

Why are start-ups risky?

The risk involved in any business start-up is due to uncertainty. Any business has to deal with uncertainty over the future. However, for business start-ups, the margin between success and failure is often very fine. Major uncertainties over the future include:

- How many customers will use our business?
- What price will customers be willing to pay?
- How often customers will return.

- What will competitors do when we open?
- Can we get the right staff?
- Will customers pay us on time?

These are perhaps just the tip of the iceberg of uncertainty and go some way towards explaining why predicting the future is always risky. If the entrepreneur has worked in the industry for some time it will be easier to have confidence in judgements involved in all these issues. It also follows that an intelligent entrepreneur is likely to learn enough from a first attempt at a new business to mean that the second attempt should be much more reliable.

Why do businesses fail?

There are several reasons why businesses fail. They are shown in the first row below, and examples are given below to illustrate:

Poor market analysis	Poor execution of a good idea	Bad luck
Failure to identify the effect an indirect competitor may have had	Poor recruitment, selection or training	Competition arrives before you open
Failure to understand what customers were looking for from your business	Purchasing the wrong stock, or the wrong amount at the wrong price	A major competitor opens up locally
Failure to understand how customers make their buying decisions	Lack of patience – panic in the face of disappointing early sales may lead to bad decisions	A major customer collapses just after you open, owing you so much cash you are forced into liquidation
You may have underestimated the loyalty of customers to your competitors	Poor cash management, e.g. paying suppliers early, but struggling to get customers to pay on time	After nine months' work, your restaurant opens its doors just as a recession is closing the doors of customers

Themes for evaluation

Does the failure to meet objectives automatically mean that a business start-up must be assessed as flawed? Entrepreneurs are natural optimists, so their overly ambitious objectives may not be met fully. Yet what if the business is still trading after the crucial first three years of existence during which so many start-ups fail? Surely that's a success. It's very important to show that you understand how difficult it is to achieve start-up success. Therefore the odd slippage from a plan should be accepted, especially if success has been achieved overall.

Exam insight

If asked to assess a start-up's success or chances of success, follow the criteria outlined above.

- Once the business has started, search your exam case study for any signs of what the business' objectives were, then look for data that confirms whether they were achieved.
- If assessing an idea before a business starts, consider carefully the typical areas of strength and weakness outlined above.

Whichever evaluative scenario you are asked to deal with, try hard to find arguments on both sides. Then come to a clear conclusion where you weigh up your arguments, based on the evidence to state whether or not the start-up was/will be successful.

Test yourself

1 Suggest one financial, one personal and one social objective for a recent local business start-up. (3)
2 In two columns, headed 'Within the entrepreneur's control' and 'Outside the entrepreneur's control', outline two reasons (in each column) why a new restaurant may fail in its first year. (8)
3 Briefly explain why each of the following could lead to business failure:
   a) delays to supplies   b) unexpected increase in costs   c) unexpected changes in demand (9)

4 Finance

Unit 16 Using budgets

What?

Budgets are agreed ceilings on spending and floors on income. If the budgets are met, the business will achieve its planned level of profit. Often the executives responsible for meeting the budgets will receive a financial bonus for success; there may even be a sliding scale of rewards, in which the bonus rises in line with success at beating the budget.

The use of budgets as a control tool relies on a process known as variance analysis. Budgeted figures are compared with actual results to identify any variance (difference) between the two figures. A difference that represents a positive result for a company's profitability is referred to as a favourable variance. A result that suggests a decline in profitability is referred to as an adverse variance (see the example in the table below). In the exam, the convention is to show favourable variances using the form £20,000F; this means a favourable variance of £20,000. Adverse variances are shown with an A.

The logic of favourable and adverse variances is quite easy to remember:

● if revenue is below budget, that's an adverse variance (bad news);
● if costs are higher than budget, that's also adverse (bad news);
● if revenue is higher than the budget, that's great (favourable variance);
● if costs are below the budgeted level, that's also great (favourable variance).

	January			February		
	Budget	Actual	Variance	Budget	Actual	Variance
Income	500	520	20F*	520	510	10A
Expenditure	400	430	30A	410	390	20F
Profits	100	90	10A	110	120	10F

* F = Favourable, A = Adverse

Commentary

In January, sales targets were surpassed (a favourable variance of 20) and, possibly as a result of the increase in sales, expenditure was also higher than expected (an adverse variance of 30).

With expenditure higher than expected the month showed an adverse variance which was big enough to outweigh the favourable income variance. This produced an adverse profit variance of 10. February was a better month, showing a favourable profit variance – as a direct result of a highly favourable total expenditure variance, i.e. cost cutting.

Meaning of variances

The simple calculation of variances shows very little in the way of clear facts. Instead, questions are posed such as: What was happening to the average selling price of the products? Was the firm able to negotiate better terms with suppliers in February (causing the favourable direct cost variance)? A variance should be seen as a trigger for further investigation, rather than an answer in itself.

Exam insight

Exam candidates often lose silly marks by forgetting the terms adverse and favourable. The examiners do *not* want the terms: positive and negative variances. It is also important to be cautious in drawing firm conclusions about praise or blame. Favourable variances may arise by chance; the manager responsible may get a bonus and lots of praise – yet have done nothing to earn it. In late 2008 HMV was struggling with the credit crunch recession – until Woolworth's closed down. Suddenly HMV CD and DVD sales pushed ahead, as Woolworth's customers had to look elsewhere. Similarly, adverse variances may be no fault of the manager who's getting all the blame! Be willing to stand up for the person concerned.

Benefits of using budgets

Budgets allow managers to practise what is known as **management by exception**. This is where they focus their attention on areas whose budgets show a large variance. This allows managers' time to be used more productively than if they were required to check every department's spending on a regular basis.

Delegating spending power to managers of separate departments may well have a motivational effect on the budget holders. Being trusted with the authority to decide how money should be spent may provide an increased feeling of responsibility.

Drawbacks of using budgets

Budgets are targets. There is no guarantee that targets will be met. Unrealistic targets may be out of reach, even if staff are working well. Staff motivation is likely to fall if unrealistic targets have been set. Meanwhile, changing objectives may require an adjustment to the business plan. Unless budgets are adjusted to account for strategic or tactical changes, targets will be irrelevant. Therefore variances need to be looked at within the bigger picture of what has been happening to the business. An adverse materials variance may have been caused by a large increase in output to meet a surge in demand.

Key Terms

Adverse variance – when actual outcomes are less favourable to profit than expected when setting the budget

Favourable variance – when actual outcomes boost profit in a way that had not been anticipated at the time of the setting the budget

Management by exception – focusing management time on departments or products that are performing particularly well or badly

Themes for evaluation

Are budgets useful for future planning? Variance analysis relies on waiting until events have actually occurred to calculate the variance. Therefore variances are always about the past, not the future. Nevertheless, if a department always seems to be over-optimistic about its sales prospects, it would be wise to cut back the budgeted figure. Variance analysis may give hints as to what needs to happen in the future but only as a result of fully investigating the past. That means investigating all the possible internal and external factors that caused the variance and deciding whether these are likely to continue to impact on the firm in the future.

Test yourself

1 Fill in the gaps in the following table. (7)

	April			May			June		
	Budget £000s	Actual £000s	Variance £000s	Budget £000s	Actual £000s	Variance £000s	Budget £000s	Actual £000s	Variance £000s
Income	500	500	0	520	530		520	510	10A
Expenditure	400	410	10A	410	410	0	410		
Profit	100	90		110	120			90	

2 Explain the meaning of the term management by exception. (3)

3 Analyse two possible causes of a new coffee shop suffering from adverse profit variances in its first few months. (6)

4 Outline two major drawbacks to a rapidly growing IT software developer relying too heavily on variance analysis to inform its planning for next year. (4)

Unit 17 Improving cash flow

What?

Cash flow is the flow of money into and out of a business in a given time period. If a business forecasts a period of negative cash flow, it should look for a business solution that does not involve debt.

Why?

Managing cash flow is about ensuring that enough cash is available to meet the cash requirements at any one time. If the bills cannot be paid on time there are serious consequences. In the worst situation the business may fail. Negative cash flow is the commonest cause of business failure. **Managing cash flow is a vital business activity.**

Managing cash flow is a continuous process. When a business starts up it takes time to generate income. Money to pay for stock and the running costs will need to be found from the initial capital invested in the business. As the business cycle gets going, income from customers will be available to pay for expenditure. The firm needs to ensure that there is always sufficient cash to meet daily requirements. If the business is expanding or takes on a special order, extra care needs to be taken to ensure that there are sufficient funds.

If cash is not controlled the business can experience problems:

- With suppliers: if payment is delayed they may reduce the length of the credit period or refuse to supply future orders.
- With banks: borrowing to cover cash shortages will result in additional interest charges. If the bank becomes concerned it may impose a higher interest rate. The firm will find it more difficult to get extra loans.
- With missed opportunities: the business may be unable to take advantage of bulk buying and the resulting lower average costs. It may have to turn down a profitable order because it does not have the necessary working capital.
- With growth: a firm that is short of working capital is unlikely to be able to grow, as no cash will be available for development.

How much?

The amount of cash that is needed varies from firm to firm. There are huge variations in the length of the business cycle. A fruit stall market trader buys supplies for cash from a wholesaler in the morning and sells everything (for cash) by late afternoon. The cycle takes less than a day. By contrast, a small construction firm building four houses may take a year between starting the project and having cash paid by a buyer.

How?

Good management of cash flow starts with good *forecasting*. Cash flow forecasts will help to predict any cash shortfalls. This will enable the business to take steps to avoid any liquidity problems.

The cash situation needs to be constantly *monitored* so that the business is not caught out by any unexpected problems.

Improving cash flow into the business

The business can improve the flow of cash into the business by:

- *Getting goods to the market in the shortest possible time* – the sooner goods reach the customer the sooner payment is received.
- *Getting paid as soon as possible* – the ideal arrangement is to get paid cash with the order or on delivery. In reality many sales are made on credit. Offering incentives such as discounts can encourage early payment.
- *Controlling debtors* – confusingly this is known as credit control. If customers do not pay on time then cash does not come into the business when expected.
- *Factoring* – it may be possible to speed up payments by factoring money owed to the business. The company receives 80 per cent of the amount due within 24 hours of an invoice being presented. The factor then collects the money from the customer when the credit period is over and pays the seller the remaining 20 per cent less the factoring fees.

Reducing cash outflows from the business

The other way of improving cash flow is to manage the outflow of cash from the business. This can be done by:

- *Obtaining maximum possible credit for purchases* – delaying payment of bills will keep cash in the business for longer.

- *Controlling costs* – this can be done by keeping administrative and production costs to a minimum.
- *Keeping stocks of raw materials to a minimum* – good stock management such as a just-in-time system means that the business is not paying for stocks before it needs them for production. Controlling stock losses means that less is spent on replacements for lost or damaged stock.

Keeping cash in the business

Cash flow can also be improved by keeping cash in the business. It could:

- *Lease rather than buy* equipment or buildings. This increases expenses but conserves capital.
- *Postpone expenditure*, e.g. on new company cars.

Exam insight

When looking at how the firm can improve its cash flow, consider the type of firm and its market situation. There is no point suggesting that the firm should demand cash payment if it is supplying large businesses in a highly competitive market.

When looking at solutions to cash flow problems it is important to consider what is causing the problem and how long the problem might go on for. There is a lot of difference between a problem caused by poor payment and one that is caused by poor sales.

Finding additional funding to cover cash shortages

If the business is unable to keep a healthy cash flow by internal management it may need to look outside to cover cash shortages. This can be done by:

- *Using an overdraft* – an overdraft allows the business to overdraw up to an agreed limit. Overdrafts usually incur high rates of interest but allow the firm to borrow only when and what it really needs. It is a very flexible form of borrowing. This makes it suitable for small or short-term shortages of cash. Although it should only be used to fund short-term problems, a recent study of firms in Bristol found that 70 per cent of small firms had a permanent overdraft. A risky aspect of an overdraft is that the bank can withdraw the facility at any time and demand instant repayment.
- *Taking out a short-term loan* – less flexible than an overdraft, short-term loans offer more security and are cheaper.
- *Sale and leaseback of assets* – if a business owns long-term assets it may be possible to negotiate a sale and leaseback arrangement. This will release capital and give an immediate inflow of cash.

Application

Dell Computer Corporation is the world's Number One personal computer manufacturer with an estimated 14 per cent of the global market. It has an enviable record of success. One factor in this success is the careful management of stock. Computers are made to the customer specification. At the assembly plant they do not keep stocks of finished machines, only component parts. After an order is received the computer is constructed then shipped to a distribution centre. Here it meets up with its various peripherals. These items such as monitors and keyboards are not held in stock but are delivered to the distribution centres directly from the suppliers.

Minimising its use of capital has helped Dell to finance and maintain its incredible growth. It has also helped the company to avoid the problems of holding stocks of computers when a change in technology makes yesterday's models obsolete and slashes their value.

Key Terms

Bad debts – payments that are long overdue and cannot be expected to be received
Capital expenditure – spending by the business on fixed assets
Credit period – the length of time allowed for payment
Liabilities – what the business owes

Themes for evaluation

Managing cash flow is about balancing company resources: too little and the firm could fail; too much and the business could miss opportunities.

It is not just about cash flow management. It is about efficiency throughout the business. It is an integrated activity. Efficient production keeps costs down and gets the goods to the customer in the shortest possible time. Good stock management reduces waste and the amount of cash tied up in stock.

Test yourself

1   What is meant by cash flow? (2)
2   What is working capital and what is it used for? Give two examples. (4)
3   Why is it important for a business to manage its cash flow? (4)
4   List two ways in which a firm can improve its cash inflows. (4)
5   Suggest two ways that a firm can solve a short-term cash flow shortage. (4)
6   What is the 'right' level of cash that a business should have available? (6)

 **Unit 18** Measuring and increasing profit

What?

Unit 11 introduced the concept of profit as the amount of revenue left over once all costs have been deducted. This unit introduces two new measurements that allow judgements to be made about a firm's profits.

Calculation 1: Net profit margin

Formula

$$\frac{\text{Net profit}}{\text{Sales revenue}} \times 100$$

Meaning

The net profit margin shows what percentage of the firm's total sales revenue is left over once all costs have been deducted. Therefore a net profit margin of 10 per cent means that 10p of every £ received from customers is net profit.

Why important?

The net profit margin indicates how much of a premium the business can charge over the total costs of production. The net profit margin is a measure of profitability – the rate at which profit is made, rather than just an absolute figure for profit. Therefore, comparisons can be made year on year, or between firms selling the same type of products. For example, Tesco's net profit margin is nearly twice as high as Sainsbury's.

	Net profit	Sales revenue	Net profit margin
Company A	£20,000	£400,000	5%
Company B	£9,000	£60,000	15%
Company C	£10,000	£100,000	10%

Superficially, Company A appears to be most successful, with a net profit of £20,000. If net profit is stated as a percentage of sales revenue (net profit margin), company B is the most efficient at generating profit, and perhaps therefore the best run company, despite its small size.

Calculation 2: Return on capital

Formula

$$\frac{\text{Net profit}}{\text{Capital invested}} \times 100$$

Meaning

This financial ratio states the return an investor receives as a percentage of what they invest. Therefore it can be directly compared with savings rates or with the same calculation for alternative uses for the money invested. This allows a judgement to be made about which use of finance offers the greatest return.

Why important?

The return on capital shows what a firm earns on its investment in clear and simple terms. It is a business version of what you would recognise as an interest rate on a savings account. The figure is therefore most useful when considering whether an investment is paying off, or whether the money put into that project would be better used elsewhere.

Exam insight

Implications

As shown by the two sections above, any attempt to increase profit usually has implications beyond just the obvious financial impact on costs or revenues. Whenever you answer a question on improving profit, be sure to develop a chain of logic within your answer that shows you are aware of the range of implications of your suggestion for increasing profit.

How to improve profitability

There are two fundamental ways to boost the profitability of a business
- *Reducing costs* – managing to generate the same level of sales revenue with lower costs will create a higher net profit margin. Sounds simple, but in fact cost reduction is rarely as simple as it sounds. Reducing a cost usually involves a trade-off, for example lowering material costs may involve reducing the quality of a product or souring relationships with a supplier. Or reducing

staffing costs could lead to lower motivation or productivity levels for the business. Moving to a cheaper location may reduce costs in the long run, but create a large extra cost in the short term as the costs of moving the operation are covered. For managers, the most attractive way to reduce costs is to increase productivity, as this means lowering the labour cost per unit. The workforce is unlikely to be as keen, though, as higher productivity means fewer jobs, unless sales are booming.

- *Raising prices* – if a business can find a way to charge more for its product without increasing its costs then increased profitability will result. However, total profit may fall as the price rise may lead to a significant fall in sales. So even though each product brings in more profit, the total amount of profit falls because of the lower level of sales. The extent to which sales change following a change in price is measured by the price elasticity of a product. This topic is covered in detail in Unit 42. For now, it is enough to remember that a price rise on a price inelastic product will increase profit. On the face of it, a price cut on a price elastic product is also likely to boost profit because, even though the profit per unit has fallen, the number of units sold has increased significantly, meaning a greater total profit. Unfortunately a price cut on a price elastic product is likely to draw a response from

competitors. If a price cut on Tetley tea leads to a price cut on PG Tips, neither business is better off.

Application: Aquasports

Aquasports is a small company, running watersport activities from two bases in the south of England. The company tries to make a profit each year, indeed financial stability is a stated objective for the firm. However, the motive behind their desire to boost profit is that it allows them to pursue their overriding purpose – of getting people hooked on the watersports that the company's owners and staff love so much. Profit is merely a way to reach out to more potential watersport converts.

Themes for evaluation

The net profit margin and return on investment help when making judgements on the success of a business. However, as we have already seen when considering the motives of entrepreneurs, or the objectives of business start-ups, profit is not always the only measure of success for a business. Some firms will consider the need to have a positive impact on the communities in which they operate. Indeed, they may see profit merely as a means to pursue other objectives.

Test yourself

1 Plowman's Potatoes Ltd is a chain of fast food outlets selling jacket potatoes with a range of fillings. The firm opened two new branches this year. Decide which new branch was the most successful by analysing the data below using the net profit margin and return on capital: (8)

	Sales revenue	Net profit	Capital invested in opening the branch
Branch X	£125,000	£25,000	£250,000
Branch Y	£200,000	£16,000	£320,000

2 Explain three different ways that a chain of DVD rental stores might cut its costs. For each, analyse one possible consequence. (9)

3 Explain why cutting price may increase profit but decrease profitability. (3)

Unit 19 Cash flow versus profit

What?

Cash flow is the flow of money through the business. Profit is the money that is left after all the costs have been paid.

Why?

It is important to distinguish between cash flow and profit, as they are important to businesses in different ways. The business world is littered with failed firms who seemed to be very profitable but still failed. Most of the time this failure was due to poor cash flow. Equally a firm can be cash rich but at the end of the day make no profit.

How?

Cash flow can be monitored by looking daily at the firm's bank account. Is there cash in the account? The formula for calculating cash flow is:

Cash flow = cash inflow – cash outflow

Profit is the excess of revenue over costs. It is normally calculated over a fixed period. Normally half yearly and annually. The formula for calculating profit is:

Profit = total revenue – total costs

Revenue is the name given to the money that a firm receives from selling the product or service that it provides. The total revenue for a firm for any given period can be calculated by multiplying the selling price (revenue per unit) by the number of units sold in that period. Revenue is one of the inflows of cash into the business but is only significant as a cash inflow when it is received.

Revenue is not the only source of cash inflows. Taking out a loan will result in cash coming into the business. Selling an old machine will also bring cash in.

Costs are the expenses associated with running the business. They can be divided into:

- Variable costs: a variable cost is one that varies in direct proportion to output. In other words, if a firm makes twice as many bags of crisps, they will need twice as many potatoes.
- Fixed costs: a fixed cost is one that does not change in relation to output. An example might be managers' salaries – they remain the same whether 10,000 or 20,000 bags of crisps are produced per month.
- Total costs: this is the figure gained by adding the total variable costs to the fixed costs.

To calculate profit the firm will look at these costs over the accounting period. For cash flow purposes costs come into the equation when the bill is paid and the money leaves the firm.

There may be other payments made by the firm such as the purchase of a new machine or the payment of dividends to shareholders. These are cash outflows but do not form part of the calculation of profit.

Why profit?

The quest for profit lies at the heart of the objectives of almost every business. The business needs to be profitable so that it can:

- Generate a return for investors. Investors put money into a business so that they get a share of the profits. A profitable business will find it easier to get investors. This will make it easier to grow and will enable it to raise funding if it has a difficult patch.
- Generate money for use in the business. Profit kept in the business is known as retained profit. This is used to buy extra assets that will help the firm in the future – perhaps extra machinery or equipment that will allow them to grow. Retained profit can also be used to bolster the firm's cash position.

The majority of businesses will actually choose to split their profit between these two uses, varying the proportion to each use depending upon their current circumstances and especially their need for extra cash either for day-to-day needs or for investment.

Why cash flow?

The business also needs to have sufficient cash available for its requirements. This includes working capital to pay for any bills that become due plus cash for any expenditure that is planned, such as buying a new machine. Failure to have sufficient cash can have serious consequences for the firm. It may face problems with suppliers, lenders and the government (if unable to pay VAT or tax bills). Any of these situations could mean that it is forced out of business by being declared insolvent.

A good healthy business will have both a good cash flow and be making profit, but there are times when a profitable company may experience cash flow problems:

- Seasonality. Some businesses experience swings in demand during the year. Garden furniture manufacturers sell most of their output in the spring as stores stock up for the summer months. This means there will be little cash coming in during the winter months but materials and staff still have to be paid for.
- Special orders. A firm may have additional cash outflows to complete a special order before it is paid.
- Expansion. The firm may have cash outflows whilst expanding until the additional revenue contributes to cash inflows.

There are also times when a cash rich business is not profitable. The business may, for example, have received huge cash inflows from the sale of shares but still not be making a profit.

Evaluation

Remember: businesses fail for two reasons – they are not profitable or they run out of cash.

A firm may be able to live with being unprofitable for a period of time but it cannot succeed if it runs out of cash. There is no such thing as negative money. Getting the balance right is what management is all about. A well-run business will be profitable and will keep its cash situation under control.

Application

In July 2009, Ocado, the online grocer, raised £40m. This takes the total financing since its start-up 10 years ago to £350m. In spite of these huge injections of cash Ocado, which has a 5-year deal to sell Waitrose products online within the M25, has never made a profit. It generates £10m of earnings each year but is unprofitable after paying interest, depreciation and tax.

Key Terms

Dividends – payments made to the shareholders out of profits.

Insolvency – when creditors force the closure of the business because it is unable to pay them

Working capital – cash available within the business to pay for day-to-day expenditure.

Exam insight

This distinction between cash flow and profit is vital in understanding how businesses work. When answering a question about either profit or cash flow be sure that you are referring to the correct concept. Remember: cash flow measures what is happening *now* to a firm's bank balance. Profit looks at the longer-term financial impact of a course of action.

Test yourself

1 What is the difference between cash inflows and revenue? (4)
2 How might seasonality affect a firm's cash flow? (4)
3 Why is it important for a new business to look at both cash flow and profitability? (8)
4 Why might a profitable business have cash flow problems? (6)

Unit 20 Integrated finance

The AQA specification for this unit says:

Candidates are expected to gain an understanding of accounting and finance in an integrated context within the organisation and the wider environment. Emphasis is placed on the use of accounting and financial information as an aid to decision making and financial control.

Three fundamental issues should be considered when revising for AS level finance: the importance of cash flow, financial monitoring and control, and making a profit.

The importance of cash flow

Why?

Never lose sight of the fact that cash flow is the only thing that will let a firm pay its bills. With no cash and bills unpaid, businesses can be forced to cease trading when their creditors take them to court to recover the unpaid debts. It is therefore vital to ensure that there is enough cash within the business to allow short-term debts to be paid when they are due.

How?

Careful financial planning should decrease the chances of cash flow problems. Cash flow forecasting is a highly effective way of focusing on the necessity of a healthy cash flow in the weeks and months to come, although it is important to remember that a cash flow forecast is never 100 per cent reliable. Since the forecast can never be wholly relied upon, problems do occur, and the various methods available to businesses to ease cash flow problems should not be overlooked.

Who?

Cash flow is more often a problem for small firms than for larger organisations. The immediacy of cash flow problems for a small firm is great – if the wages are not paid, no one turns up for work next week. However, even the very largest firms can fall victim to cash flow problems (as Woolworth's did in 2008). Those that over-borrow in order to finance growth will find heavy interest payments a substantial drain on cash flow.

What it's not

Cash flow is not the same as profit. Profit is not cash, and sales do not mean immediate cash inflows.

The most significant cause of differences between cash flow and profit is credit sales. A sale is made, recorded as such and a profit recorded on that sale. However, most firms sell to other businesses on credit – perhaps allowing them as long as three months to pay. In this case, the firm may not be able to bridge the gap between cash outflows (spent making the product) and the inflows that will only arrive once the customer pays up.

Financial monitoring and control

Why?

Tight financial controls are needed in business to keep fixed overhead costs down and to ensure that variable costs stay in line with revenues. Achieving this level of financial efficiency is the role of the managers who have been set budgets to monitor their own department's finances.

How?

A budgeting system is the vehicle through which firms are able to delegate spending power to managers. Centrally determined budgets allow clear control over planned expenditures. Variance analysis should ensure that potential problems can be identified early enough to be dealt with.

Monitoring the finances of the business is the only sensible way to ensure that decision makers can continue to make informed decisions that will allow the business to make a satisfactory profit.

Making a profit

What?

Any business featured in an exam question will be concerned with the amount of profit it generates. It is therefore critical to develop a thorough understanding of the concept. Generating or increasing profit will come from boosting revenues and/or cutting costs. Profitability is subtly different to profit. Profitability measures the proportion of revenue that the firm can turn into profit (as a percentage), whereas profit is an absolute value, measured in pounds.

To sum it up:

- profit is a sum of money, e.g. £20 000;
- profitability is a relative term, e.g. 10 per cent (10p profit for every £1 of sales).

Integrated finance

Naturally, big businesses are likely to make more profit than small businesses; but is their profitability higher? Knowing the difference between profit and profitability allows you to write accurately and analytically.

How?

Reading student answers to finance questions can often lead an examiner to question why any business fails. There is a tendency to assume that any firm can cut its costs at any time without any significant reduction in its performance. Think again.

- Reducing material costs may hit product quality.
- Cutting wages or shedding staff will demotivate the workforce.
- Moving to a cheaper location involves huge short-term costs, disruption and general upheaval involved in shifting an entire business (especially a manufacturer).

If profit were easy, how could any business struggle?

Evaluation

Finance is only a support function within a business. Those whose roles involve planning, monitoring and evaluating financial performance do not make anything or generate any profit. If businesses exist to make a profit, then the role of the finance people is simply to measure success. It is the marketing people who come up with the ideas and the operations staff who create the products and services being sold. Managing these people, getting the most out of them and any equipment they may be using, as well as effectively communicating your company's message to customers are what will make a firm successful. Of course finance departments have a key role to play in advising these other areas of the firm, but a business is more than just a set of numbers.

Exam insight

Finance questions may need you to make calculations. These calculations are not mathematical challenges – they will test your ability to apply business studies knowledge. Try to ensure a full mastery of any financial calculations you may be required to make (break-even analysis, profit and profit margin calculations, cash flow forecasts and budget variances). The big marks, however, tend to come from being able to show a written understanding of the importance of financial matters to the running of a business.

Test yourself

1. Analyse the potential benefits to a firm from effective financial monitoring. (5)
2. Explain why financial forecasts can never be 100 per cent reliable. (5)
3. Outline two possible solutions to a cash flow crisis caused by a short-term dip in sales for a crisp manufacturer. (4)
4. Explain why cash flow may be more important than profit to a firm that is expanding. (6)
5. Fill in the blanks on the following cash flow forecast: (10)

	January	February	March
Cash in	100	110	120
Cash out	90	110	130
Net cash flow		0	
Opening balance	10		
Closing balance			

6. Identify two benefits of cash flow forecasting. (2)
7. Explain what is meant by the term 'factoring'. (3)
8. Briefly explain how improved working capital control can aid cash flow. (4)
9. State three internal sources of finance. (3)
10. Identify one long-term source of finance only available to limited companies. (1)
11. State the formula for calculating return on capital for an investment project. (2)
12. Explain the difference between profit and profitability. (3)
13. State two limitations of break-even analysis. (2)

Now have a go at these data response questions. You should allow yourself 30 minutes for each.

Data response: Celebration Cakes

L&H Davison Ltd, manufacturers of high-quality baked goods has seen significant recent success following a deal with several major supermarket chains. The company is to supply celebration cakes featuring popular children's TV and film characters. Success has come rapidly for the firm which has been struggling to meet the extra orders. Anna Prickett, the firm's finance director, has drawn up the following figures relating to a proposal to rent extra factory space. This would be dedicated to meeting the orders from the supermarkets, leaving the firm's existing production facilities to cope with existing customers and smaller scale new business.

Average selling price (price paid by supermarket)	£2.60
Variable cost per cake	£0.80
Rent on extra factory space (per month)	£44,000
Other extra overheads (per month)	£28,000

Worried about the bargaining power of the supermarket chains, L&H Davison Ltd is unwilling to purchase extra premises or machinery. It is therefore renting all the equipment needed. This means that the only extra finance needed is an estimated £80,000 to fund the extra day-to-day costs. This will be necessary because of the generous credit terms offered to the supermarkets, and the inability of L&H Davison Ltd to negotiate longer credit terms with its own suppliers. L&H Davison's Managing Director, Chaz Simpson, has expressed concern over the strained cash flow position that will be created by accepting this new business from the supermarkets. Cash flow forecasts suggest that the firm will have to endure several months of negative net cash flows in the near future.

Questions

1 Outline two internal sources of finance that could be used to generate the extra working capital required. (4)
2 Calculate the expected break-even output of the new factory for Celebration Cakes. (4)
3 Analyse one reason why this break-even analysis may prove unreliable. (6)
4 Discuss the possible solutions to L&H Davison Ltd's cash flow problems relating to the supermarket orders. (9)

Data response: Nurwoo Noodles

Nurwoo Ltd is in the rapidly expanding noodle market. The firm's no-frills approach to Chinese fast food has allowed for rapid expansion in its five-year history. It now has eight restaurants operating in South East London and Kent. The founder of the business, Mr Woo, oversees the operations of the firm but the manager of each restaurant is responsible for hitting budgets agreed with the founders on a six-monthly basis. With financial data analysed separately for each restaurant, the founders are growing concerned over the performance of the Bromley branch, managed by Ben Greenhalgh. Recruited straight from university, Ben oversaw the successful opening of the restaurant in January 2009. Since then, performance has dipped. Ben has been called to a meeting with Mr Woo to explain the budget statement shown below for July–December 2009 at the Bromley restaurant:

	Budgeted (£)	Actual (£)
Eat-in sales	16,000	11,200
Take-away sales	20,000	19,500
Total revenue	36,000	30,700
Ingredients	12,000	10,500
Wages	13,800	13,600
Overheads	6,000	6,900
Total costs	31,800	31,000

Questions

1 Explain the meaning of the term 'total revenue'. (2)
2 Calculate the profit variance for Bromley for the period July–December 2009. (4)
3 Calculate the expected and actual net profit margin for the Bromley branch for the period July-December 2009. (4)
4 Analyse one reason for keeping the Bromley restaurant open. (5)
5 To what extent would tighter budgetary control have prevented problems at the Bromley branch? (9)

5 People in business

Unit 21 Productivity and performance

What?

Productivity measures the efficiency with which a firm turns input into output. The commonest type of productivity measured is labour productivity: output per worker.

Productivity – not output

Productivity is not the same as total output. Productivity measures output per employee. One firm may have a higher output than another, yet a lower rate of productivity. If this is the case, the smaller, more efficient firm is likely to prove more successful in the long term.

Why?

The more units of output each employee produces, the lower the labour cost per unit (unless they are paid purely on piece rate). Higher productivity creates lower input costs per unit which means a lower total cost and a more competitive business. It is therefore able to charge lower prices, or generate more profit per unit, than its less productive rivals. Productivity is therefore a hugely important variable for many firms. Managers will focus a great deal of time and energy on finding methods of raising productivity.

Different measures of productivity

There are different measures of productivity, as shown in the following table:

Context	Measure of productivity
Manufacturer	Units of output per worker per week
Supermarket	Average number of items
Checkout	'Zapped' per minute
Call centre	Calls answered per hour
Fruit picking	Kilograms per day
Insurance company	Number of claims processed per week

Why not?

The problem with productivity is that it's such a powerful idea that it can be misused. Is efficiency always a good thing? A head teacher (or government) might want education to be more efficient. So, instead of 16 students per A-level class, why not 32? That would double the teacher's productivity. In effect, the same number of students could be taught by half the number of teachers, saving money and taxes. Clearly productivity is a purely quantitative measure; some qualitative measures (such as quality of homework marking) may be important, but much harder to measure.

A further problem comes from people doing jobs for which there is no realistic (or safe) measurement. What if surgeons were measured on their productivity? What if they felt pressured to do three heart operations per day? What if a medical complication required extra time; would the surgeon feel pressured into hurrying?

How?

Increasing productivity

1 *Training* – better trained staff will be capable of working faster and more accurately. Better quality means that fewer materials will be needed to produce the same output, and a higher rate of productivity due to less time wasted correcting mistakes.
2 *Motivation* – a more motivated workforce is likely to work harder and in a more focused manner, showing commitment to the job. Staff are also more likely to come up with ideas for improving productivity levels.
3 *Management* – organisation of the workplace and the production process can be a crucial factor in achieving higher levels of efficiency. Management may also encourage staff to share their ideas for improving productivity.
4 *Technology* – more advanced machinery and equipment can speed up processes – allowing higher levels of output, reduced levels of labour and time input.

What next?

With higher productivity more units of output can be produced at a lower cost per unit. This provides the opportunity to increase sales by cutting price.

Higher productivity also allows output levels to rise without taking on any extra staff. If a firm had been struggling to meet demand, this is great news. So rising productivity is especially valuable to firms with products in the growth stages of their life cycle, or at times when economic growth is boosting demand.

On the other hand, firms may decide that there is unlikely to be any significant extra demand for their product and take the opportunity to reduce their workforce. The same number of units can now be produced by fewer staff. This course of action has significant implications in terms of employee job security and levels of trust between management and staff. A more positive alternative would be to find some other way to use the staff no longer needed for their original purpose: to redeploy them to a new task. This alternative is clearly preferable to redundancy, as far as staff are concerned.

Fig. 21A: Productivity diagram

Application

Faster inquiries

In 2003 the new directory inquiry service 118 118 set up a bonus system based upon the speed with which operators answered calls. This gave staff a financial incentive to increase their productivity. In response, some staff gave out wrong numbers or just put the phone down on customers, in order to keep within the deadline for their bonuses. When this was uncovered by journalists, 118 118 suffered embarrassing publicity and made 30 staff redundant. This shows that boosting productivity must be handled with care.

Slower food

Market research by McDonald's demonstrated the limitations of a total focus on increased productivity, with customers complaining that staff were rushing their orders and not paying enough attention to satisfying customers. McDonald's moved the focus of their staff away from speed (customers served per hour) towards customer satisfaction (happy customers per hour?).

Themes for evaluation

Managers can make the mistake of seeing high productivity as an end in itself. Yet it is important to consider the effects of achieving a higher level of productivity. Increasing productivity can bring fears of redundancy unless the firm is in a position to increase output. This can damage the relationship between staff and managers, especially if managers are seen a slave drivers, continually pushing for higher levels of productivity.

Other negative side effects may evolve as a result of attempts to boost productivity. Any increase in productivity that leads to quality problems may well be a major problem. Employees rushing to finish more work in a given time may be forced to cut corners in their jobs, leading to poorer quality standards. Simply encouraging employees to work faster is likely to cause deep problems relating to the firm's reputation with its customers. Firms that pride themselves on customer service may suffer as a result of frantic attempts to increase productivity, with staff rushing through their dealings with customers in an attempt to serve more customers per hour. In both cases attempts to increase productivity may damage the firm's overall performance.

Test yourself

1 Calculate the output per worker of a firm with a workforce of 500 that manufactures 20,000 units per month. (2)
2 Identify the four main routes to increasing productivity. (4)
3 Outline two potential benefits of achieving a higher level of productivity on supermarket checkouts. (6)
4 Explain how a drive to increase productivity may result in employee dissatisfaction. (8)

Unit 22 Organisational structure

What?

The structure of an organisation shows the formal relationships between the staff within a business.

NB: Check that you understand the key terms listed at the end of this unit before starting your revision of organisations.

Why?

The people within an organisation need to identify who to go to for advice, who is their boss and who they are in charge of. A formal structure makes these issues clear and helps the people within an organisation to understand what authority they have and who they are accountable to. Most businesses follow the traditional approach to organisational structure, in which:

● everyone is answerable to a single boss, who is clearly identified on the organisational chart;
● no manager is responsible for too many – or too few – staff, i.e. the normal span of control is around 3 – 6 people;
● the overall structure of the organisation is kept stable for long periods of time (decades, perhaps), so that each division of the business develops its own management style.

How?

Designing a structure

Organisations have traditionally been hierarchically structured, that is the structure resembles a pyramid with the highest levels of authority at the top of the pyramid and power flowing downwards to the lower, wider, levels within the structure.

Functional or divisional hierarchies

These hierarchies are split into separate sections within the business. A functional structure sets out a hierarchy for the people within that function – so, for example, there will be a marketing director in charge of the whole marketing department. Divisional structures split the organisation into different sections according to the different products made by the company or the different geographical locations, so a major multinational may have separate divisions for Europe, the Americas and Asia – each with its own boss.

Hierarchical structures can vary significantly in their shape, with some companies preferring a flat structure with few layers of hierarchy and wide spans of control. Other firms prefer a structure with narrow spans of control – this will lead to the appearance of a tall, thin structure.

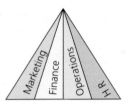
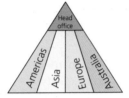

Fig 22A: Functional hierarchy/divisional structure

Advantages of a flat structure	Advantages of a tall structure
Encourages delegation	Allows far greater control
Reduces distance from senior management to shop-floor staff	Less likelihood of mistakes, as supervision is tighter
Encourages bottom-up communication	Better promotional prospects

Who?

Different businesses will find differing structures more appropriate.
● A tall structure would be particularly effective when most staff are unskilled or inexperienced, perhaps part-time or temporary, or where the smallest mistake can have huge consequences, such as in the design and production of aircraft components.
● A flat structure would be useful when highly skilled staff should be encouraged to take their own decisions or when market trends are rapidly changing.

Centralised or decentralised power

These differing shapes of structure can also be described by referring to where the decision-making power tends to lie. A tall structure tends to keep authority in one place – at the higher levels of the structure – and is therefore referred to as centralised. A decentralised structure is one where power is spread throughout the organisation, with even lower levels of staff empowered to make decisions that concern their own jobs. Such a phenomenon is more likely to be found in a flatter structure.

How else?

Matrix

A matrix structure is one where lines of authority run both vertically and horizontally. Superimposed on top of a traditional functional structure are project teams set up to work on a particular project that is current to the firm's needs. These project teams will include people from whichever departments are necessary – perhaps someone from marketing, someone from finance, an engineer and a couple of scientists might be working on developing a new product line.

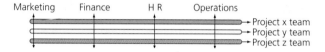

Fig 22B: Matrix management

Informal

In small businesses there may be no formal organisational structure. The 'boss' may not have set up layers of management hierarchy. In this circumstance it is likely that an informal power structure will have built up, probably based on how long staff have worked there. The lack of structure might be unsettling for a new, perhaps young, member of staff. It is nice to know who is formally responsible for what; no one wants to tread on another person's toes – especially without knowing it.

Themes for evaluation

The right structure for the organisation

Firms have control over their organisational structures. With this in mind, it is important for a company to ensure that the structure it has in place suits the staff within the firm and the operations of the business. Different structures have different strengths and the directors of any organisation should decide which are the key features that suit their particular position and which structure best meets their needs.

Changing the structure

Changing an organisation's structure can be a theme within exam case studies and can be viewed (at least superficially) as a tough job. Structural change, as with any major change within an organisation can cause uncertainty, even fear. During the economic downturn in 2008 and 2009 some firms used 'delayering'. This meant eliminating a whole management layer from a hierarchy, usually by making experienced managers redundant. In recent years some firms have looked at closing whole divisions. Whatever long-term benefits might stem from a flatter hierarchy or slimmed down organisation, in the short term the key is to manage the change effectively and sympathetically.

Exam insight

Successful exam answers require precise knowledge of the terminology involved in organisational structures. Only then will an examiner be convinced that the student understands the issues raised by the firm's organisational hierarchy.

It is crucial to be aware of the implications that certain structural types and shapes carry for the way in which the business is run. Consider how the working experience might differ if you move from a firm with a matrix structure to one with a tall hierarchical structure.

Key Terms

Accountability – identifying who an employee is answerable to, and for what

Authority – the power to make decisions over what to do and how to do it

Chain of command – the vertical lines of authority within a structure

Functions – the major types of activity necessary for a firm to function, e.g. marketing, finance, personnel (human resources), operations

Span of control – the number of subordinates for whom a manager is directly responsible

Test yourself

1 Explain what is meant by the following terms:
   a) wide span of control
   b) long chain of command
   c) centralised structure. (6)
2 Outline two benefits to an advertising agency of ensuring that its structure is flat. (4)
3 Briefly outline two possible problems of a matrix structure. (6)
4 Explain two benefits of ensuring that an organisation has a clear organisational structure that all staff understand. (4)

Unit 23 Measuring the effectiveness of the workforce

What?

Measuring workforce effectiveness means judging how well a workforce is performing, using measures such as absence levels and productivity/efficiency. This can help decisions about human resource management. If objective, quantifiable information can be used, decisions on changes to personnel policies and practices can be based on fact rather than guesswork.

As with every other aspect of business, there is scope for arguments between those who believe in quantification and those who have their doubts. The problem of using any type of quantified measurement is that it tends to distort the thing being measured. For example, if students' A Level marks were purely based on the number of words written in the time available, 'productivity' would rise, but quality would virtually disappear.

How?

You need to know of two different measures of workforce effectiveness – labour productivity and labour turnover. What you need to know is summarised in the table below.

Labour productivity

A slower rate of output from staff will mean that costs per unit go up and cause problems for the firm due to the need to push up prices. This would make the business less competitive, or force it to accept a lower profit margin on each unit of output. Solving a productivity problem is often not as easy as it may seem on the surface, since problems with employee motivation are usually deep-rooted and hard to uncover and rectify. Meanwhile, productivity problems caused by poor equipment or machinery are likely to require significant investment. This may be hard to find when the firm's profitability is being damaged by poor productivity.

Classic quotes on productivity

'Management that is destructively critical when mistakes are made kills initiative and it's essential that we have many people with initiative if we're to continue to grow.'

Lewis Lehr, President of the US 3M company

'It takes five years to develop a new car in this country. Heck, we won World War II in four years.'

Ross Perot, Founder of EDS (major US software company)

Name and description	Formula	Causes of problems	Consequences of problems
Labour productivity – a measure of how effectively employees produce units of output	$$\frac{\text{Output per period}}{\text{Average no of employees per period}}$$	Motivation, management style, lack of capital investment, inadequate resources	Increased cost per unit since labour costs are spread over fewer units, leading to a lack of competitiveness
Labour turnover – measures how many staff have left the business during a time period	$$\frac{\text{No of staff who left work}}{\text{Average total staffing level}} \times 100$$	Lack of motivation which may be caused by cultural, management style or hygiene issues. Hasty or ill-considered recruitment. Inadequate pay or fringe benefits	Extra costs of recruitment and training of new staff, along with disruption to production. Some labour turnover can be beneficial as it can bring new ideas into the business

Labour turnover

Clearly losing too many staff creates problems for a business. However, a little labour turnover is usually viewed as a good way of bringing in new ideas and expertise. Breaking down labour turnover figures may be useful, since labour turnover caused by retirement is not likely to indicate any significant problems. It is important to know what proportion of labour turnover was caused by dissatisfaction with the job. Therefore most businesses carry out 'exit interviews' with staff – to find out why they are leaving.

Labour turnover is also affected by 'natural wastage' caused by people leaving to have a family or go off to travel the world. As the term suggests, there is not much that a management can do to avoid labour turnover caused by natural wastage.

Classic quotes on labour turnover

'Cutting labour turnover helps boost sales turnover.'

Chief executive, U.S. clothing store chain

'Retention efforts may be time-consuming, but not as troublesome as turnover.'

Dave Wilmer, CEO Robert Half Technology

Application

Research on Labour turnover on the UK

Brunel University Professor Christopher Martin's findings on labour turnover in the twenty-first century reveal that the UK's average labour turnover rate is around 12.5 per cent. However, in certain types of firm, rates are far higher. He points to three categories as being of particular concern:
- firms that employ highly skilled labour;
- firms that provide a significant amount of training for their staff;
- firms in 'high-tech' sectors.

His main advice is to ensure that effective communication helps to build a mission to which all staff can commit.

Key Terms

Natural wastage – the rate at which staff leave for natural reasons such as retirement or parenthood.
Productivity – efficiency, often measured as output per worker.

Themes for evaluation

The key issue behind this unit is the attempt to quantify the people management function of a business. Measures of workforce performance such as those discussed here give objective (scientific) evidence on issues that can seem quite woolly. Many managers only really treat quantifiable issues as important. In this context, people management issues may be overlooked unless the tools to quantify them are in use. These measures therefore allow a firm to evaluate its management policies and foster a culture of continuous improvement, not just in the way that products are made but also in the way that people are managed.

It is important to avoid seeing these numbers as an answer. Just as budget variances indicate further areas for exploration, so the measures of workforce effectiveness simply raise questions. A high staff turnover may have a wide range of causes. These need further investigation. Be clear that these numbers ask questions, they do not answer them.

Exam insight

Carefully examine the information provided in the case study when answering written questions on measuring workforce performance. It is the other information within the case study that will indicate the probable causes of any problems for this business, and also probably hint at appropriate solutions to the problems.

Test yourself

1 Analyse the data shown below for a small bicycle manufacturer called Weavers and Weavers Ltd. Build up your answer by analysing the trend, possible causes and possible effects: (8)

	This year	Last year	2 years ago
Labour productivity (units per worker per week)	32	32	35
Labour turnover (%)	23	18	12

2 Explain why it may be useful to distinguish between natural wastage and labour turnover. (4)
3 Analyse why it may be hard to measure the quality of a firm's people management in a meaningful way. (8)

Unit 24 Recruitment and training

What?

The terms recruitment and selection describe the whole process involved in appointing a new member of staff. Recruitment specifically refers to what goes on up to the point that applications for the post are received. Once applications are in, the selection process then deals with choosing which applicants will be appointed.

Typical process for hiring a new employee

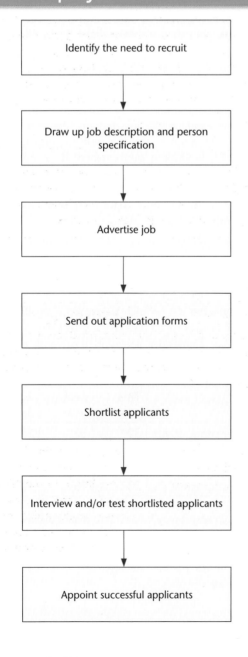

How?

Staff may be recruited internally (existing employees) or externally.

Benefits of internal recruitment	Benefits of external recruitment
• Firm already knows member of staff – lessens danger of a disastrous appointment being made • The member of staff already understands the firm's culture • Induction training will not be necessary	• There will be a far wider pool of applicants to choose from • New staff may bring in fresh ideas from outside the company

Two key documents

The job description and person specification are the two key documents used when recruiting staff. The job description covers what responsibilities and tasks will be involved in the job. The person specification describes the type of skills, experience and personal qualities that the ideal candidate for the job should possess. The person specification is crucial to the selection process, since the applicant that best matches the person specification should be the ideal candidate for the job.

Selection

One or more of the following methods of selection may be employed.
- *Application forms* – used to draw up a shortlist.
- *Interview* – ranges from informal five minutes to interviews that can last several days for more senior members of staff.
- *Psychometric tests* – allow a firm to assess the attitudes held by applicants: this can help to ensure that the recruit will fit into the firm's culture.
- *Aptitude tests* – test the actual skills of the employee; usually mental reasoning skills rather than hands-on practical skills.
- *Role plays* – can allow firms to assess the way that recruits might react in a range of different work scenarios.

Interviews, psychometric tests, aptitude tests and role plays may all take place in one specialist location, known as an assessment centre.

Who?

Job	Recruitment method
Temporary fruit picker	Application form (perhaps); possibly a very brief, informal chat with the boss
Retail store manager	Application forms and CVs will be requested, then shortlisted candidates will probably be required to take part in a whole day of interviews, including various types of testing and possibly some role play activities
Finance director	Adverts appearing in the *Financial Times* may attract a number of applicants who will be shortlisted on the basis of CV and reputation. The shortlisted applicants are likely to undergo a rigorous series of interviews and tests, quite possibly over several days. This process may well be handled by a specialist (and expensive) recruitment consultant

Training

Training may be used to fulfil the following needs:

1. The need to introduce new staff to the firm's systems and procedures. This is known as induction training.
2. The desire to increase the range of skills available within the firm to allow for flexibility or future changes.
3. To increase the knowledge and commitment to the firm of the workforce.
4. To enhance the quality of work produced by staff.
5. Note that some employers would be inclined to train staff for life as well as for the job, that is offer training for personal development such as a foreign language and courses in public speaking or assertiveness. Other employers are more likely to focus upon skills related directly to the job in hand.

On or off the job?

On the job training involves training staff while they are actively involved in the job they are being trained to do. Typically, an experienced employee will sit with the trainee, explaining what needs to be done and giving feedback on their performance and how they can improve. Off the job training takes the employee away from their job (maybe to a training room elsewhere in the building or even off-site or at a college) and delivering the training there.

Exam insight

Be clear about the difference between an exam question on 'recruitment' and a question on 'selection'. Examiners treat 'recruitment' as the stages up to but *not* including selection.

On the job training		Off the job training	
Advantages	Disadvantages	Advantages	Disadvantages
Trainee learns on the equipment they are going to be using with familiar colleagues around making training totally relevant	It may be hard to concentrate on training in the working environment with the normal stresses and pressures of the job to contend with	Allows time for reflection and questioning without the day-to-day pressures of the workplace	Lost production time as the employee is taken away from their post
Production time is not lost as the trainee is still working	Trainees may miss the opportunity to take a more reflective and questioning approach to their training	More likely to be delivered by a professional trainer	May rely on simulation or slightly different equipment or machinery, meaning the employee has to make adjustments when they get back to their own workstation

Exam insight

Questions on training often offer the perfect opportunity to construct a relatively sophisticated line of analysis in your answer. With the concept of motivation so clearly linked to training, the chance to use a motivation theorist to explain why training may motivate staff, or a lack of training may demotivate them, is too good to pass up.

Themes for evaluation

Effective recruitment and training brings a number of benefits to firms. However, there is no question that certain aspects of recruitment and training will actually increase costs in the short term. Training can be expensive, yet in the medium to long term it can enhance productivity and therefore reduce costs. It may also improve staff motivation and reduce labour turnover, further reducing costs. The attitude of senior managers towards their staff is likely to be the key factor in deciding how seriously those benefits are set against the obvious costs. Look for indicators within a case study as to management attitudes towards staff before judging their approach to managing their people.

Key Terms

External recruitment – filling a job vacancy by bringing in someone new to the business

Induction training – training that introduces new staff to the firm's systems and procedures when they join the company

Internal recruitment – filling a job vacancy with a current employee

Job description – a document that lists the main roles and responsibilities attached to a job

Off the job training – occurs when employees gain skills in an environment away from their normal workstation

On the job training – occurs when employees gain skills while engaged in their normal job

Person specification – a document describing the attributes of the ideal candidate for a job

Test yourself

1 Explain what is meant by the terms:
   a) external recruitment (3)
   b) selection (3)
2 Outline two reasons why a casual labourer may be selected without the use of an interview. (4)
3 Briefly explain what factors may affect the choice of whether to offer on the job or off the job training to a supermarket employee learning to use a new till. (5)
4 Analyse the potential benefits to staff of being trained to take on new, more demanding roles at work. (5)

Unit 25 Motivation in theory

What?

The question of what motivates people to work has been studied formally for most of the last 100 years. There are four key motivation theorists with whose work you may be familiar: F. W. Taylor, Elton Mayo, Abraham Maslow and Frederick Herzberg. You must know at least one of these theories very well – ideally an understanding of all four gives you a better chance to find a theory to explain what you read about in your exam case studies.

F. W. Taylor

What did he say?

Taylor was admittedly more than just a motivation theorist, concentrating on how work should be organised. Working in the period 1890–1920, Taylor's work was rooted in his belief that the only factor that motivates people to work is money.

How to organise the workplace

- *High division of labour* – Taylor felt that any production process should be split into as many separate tasks as possible. This allowed for the identification of small simple jobs that could be repeated over and over again. This allowed unskilled workers to become specialists in that job very quickly and thus achieve high rates of output with virtually no training or experience. In recent years McDonald's in America announced a plan to have zero training, that is to hire new staff and put them to work immediately (it later abandoned this Taylorite scheme).
- *Payment by results* – Taylor favoured piece rate, in other words paying per unit produced. He believed that this would encourage people to work hard without the need for tight supervision. All a supervisor would need to do is to count the quantity of work produced.
- *Time and motion study* – Taylor advocated taking a scientific approach to organising work. He studied the way work was done and identified the 'one best way' to do the job. Each part of the job could be timed to identify how much each worker should be expected to achieve in a day. This could then be used to set challenging piece rate targets.
- *Best tools for the job* – a key part of Taylor's scientific approach was to ensure that his workers were given

tools that were designed carefully to make their job as straightforward as possible, thus speeding up production.

Elton Mayo

What did he say?

Mayo was originally a keen advocate of Taylor's ideas and his most famous set of experiments were designed to examine Taylor's theories. The results of the 'Hawthorne experiments' led Mayo to take motivation theory a step forward. The research showed that factors other than money could impact on the motivation of staff. This altered the way that many firms treated their staff.

How to organise the workplace

- *Teamworking* – Mayo identified the importance of 'group norms'. A team could work together for the good of all, or be obstructive and negative. Taylor thought of workers as individuals; Mayo saw the importance of managing their team spirit.
- *Social facilities* – since workers work better if they feel part of a team, any opportunity should be taken to encourage this feeling of togetherness. Social facilities or sports clubs at the workplace are examples of ways in which firms have tried to develop this feeling of belonging.
- *Hawthorne effect* – this describes the beneficial impact on staff work rate and morale of managers taking an active personal interest in their staff. You have probably already seen this in action at school – you worked harder for teachers who actually seemed to care about what and how you were doing. Likewise in the workplace – if the boss is interested in what you're doing, this provides a boost to morale and performance.

Exam insight

The first step to success is to know the work of these theorists exactly – vague references to motivation theorists add little to an answer. The best approach is to choose one relevant theorist and use the theory to analyse the business situation in detail. Avoid briefly saying: 'Taylor would say this, Mayo would say that and…'

Abraham Maslow

What did he say?

Maslow's hierarchy, shown below, identifies five types of need that human beings will try to satisfy. Knowledge of these needs should encourage a manager to apply them to the workplace (see the table 'How to apply Maslow to the workplace' on the next page).

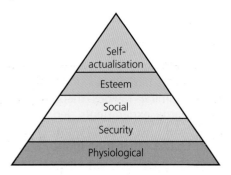

Fig 25A: Maslow's hierarchy of needs

Frederick Herzberg

What did he say?

Herzberg's two-factor theory suggests that there are two groups of factors that affect job satisfaction: 'motivators' such as responsibility can lead to positive job satisfaction; 'hygiene factors' such as working conditions can remove or cause job dissatisfaction, but have no potential for causing lasting job satisfaction. The identification of factors that determine workers' levels of job satisfaction and dissatisfaction allows managers to get the highest possible level of performance from staff. Herzberg's two different sets of factors determining motivation are shown in the table below.

Hygiene factors (remove dissatisfaction)	Motivators (provide positive job satisfaction)
Company policy and administration	Achievement
Supervisor's competence	Recognition for achievement
Salary	Work itself
Relations with supervisor	Responsibility
Working conditions	Psychological growth and advancement

How to motivate workers

Herzberg's advice in bitesize chunks is as follows:
1 Address both hygiene factors and motivators – poor hygiene means unhappy staff, weak motivators leads to an 'acceptable' (but no more) level of performance.
2 Jobs should be designed to allow workers to learn and grow.
3 A job should involve the opportunity to produce a complete unit of work (finish a whole project or produce a whole product from start to finish).
4 The process of designing jobs to include as many motivators as possible was what Herzberg referred to as 'job enrichment'.

Criticisms of the theorists

Theorist	Criticisms
Taylor	There's far more to it than money. Repetitive jobs and piece rate can lead to quality problems, boredom, resentment and high labour turnover
Mayo	Mayo's views were radical, even revolutionary, but managers turned his theory into bland ideas such as social clubs and football teams at work
Maslow	Does everyone have the same five-stage hierarchy, or are some people satisfied to work for money and a good time with their mates, i.e. uninterested in stretching themselves?
Herzberg	Theory based on research conducted amongst accountants and engineers – is the theory applicable to other types of job?

Themes for evaluation

Can any theory explain human behaviour at work?

There are likely to be so many different variables that influence workplace performance that any attempt at a single explanation of motivation may be doomed to failure. This argument would suggest that every single individual must be treated differently according to their own personal situation.

How many people actually know about this?

Few of those responsible for managing people at work have actually spent any time studying motivation theory. More advanced theories – such as Herzberg's two-factor theory – may therefore be completely ignored in many workplaces. In a few lucky instances managers may have a natural feeling for what is likely to motivate their staff, yet many tend to assume that money is enough. In these cases, staff may not give their best and therefore a key resource is being underused. It could be argued that motivation theories are the most important piece of business knowledge available to managers.

How to apply Maslow to the workplace

Hierarchy	In a work context	Role of manager
Self-actualisation	Develop new skills	Implement a training programme and create challenging assignments for staff
Esteem	Recognition, status, power	Praise staff who achieve, offer promotions and/or bonuses
Social	Opportunities for teamwork	Create a team environment with effective communication systems and social facilities to allow staff to mix after work
Security or safety	Job security	Clear job description, simple lines of accountability – just one boss
Physical or physiological	Adequate pay and breaks should ensure a worker's physiological needs are met	Appropriate pay, breaks and comfortable physical working conditions

Key Terms

Division of labour – splitting a process into small, simple, repetitive jobs

Job enrichment – designing a job to include as many of Herzberg's motivators as possible

Piece rate – paying people per piece of work they complete, e.g. 50p per pair of sewn jeans

Time and motion study – watching the way a process is completed and identifying standard times for each section of the process to be completed in order to identify the best way and expected time for that process

Test yourself

1 Identify three modern business practices that flowed from the work of F. W. Taylor. (3)
2 Outline two pieces of advice that Mayo might give to new managers, explaining how each would help to bring the best out of their staff. (4)
3 Briefly explain how each of Maslow's sets of needs might be achieved in the workplace. (10)
4 For each of the following, identify whether Herzberg classed it as a motivator or a hygiene factor:
   a) salary
   b) recognition for achievement
   c) relationship with supervisor (3)

Unit 26 Motivation in practice

What?

Job enrichment

Herzberg's prescription for motivating staff is to provide them with what he termed **job enrichment**. An enriched job has several key features:

1 *A complete unit of work* – each employee should be able to see their work as contributing to the production of a complete and identifiable finished product.
2 *Direct feedback* – a worker should know how they are doing without someone else needing to tell them. There should be no need for a quality control inspector.
3 *Direct communication* – if a worker needs to talk to anyone in another department, they should be permitted to do so, without needing to go through traditional channels of communication.

How?

Some examples of how to enrich a job are illustrated in the table below.

What else?

Other means of motivating staff include job enlargement, **empowerment**, teamworking and financial reward systems.

Job enlargement

This is the process of building a wider range of tasks into a job, possibly including a variety of tasks with different levels of responsibility. This can allow employees to grow within their working lives, enabling

them to feel a sense of self-actualisation. However, job enlargement is frequently used as a euphemism for increasing the workload of staff without making their jobs any more interesting.

Empowerment

Empowerment means passing genuine decision-making power to a worker – not just how to do a job but to decide exactly what job needs doing. Such an initiative usually requires deep-rooted cultural change since managers need to trust in the instincts and skills of their staff. A genuine theory Y manager should be able to operate a system of empowerment effectively. Managers who are unwilling to trust their staff completely will fail to see the benefits of empowerment, since staff will always feel they are being checked up on or over-supervised.

Teamworking

Introducing a system where groups of employees are split into identifiable teams. These teams work together to improve performance within their area of the firm and are held responsible for the level of performance they produce. Though this approach undoubtedly helps to meet employees' social needs, other benefits are expected, such as better problem-solving performance since the team can pool their ideas.

Exam insight

Will you be able to spot a case study where the management are saying the right things but failing to act in a way that reflects what they are saying? Too often in exam questions, students take an uncritical approach to considering motivational tools. Be willing to be critical.

	Job enrichment in a manufacturing plant	Job enrichment in a clothes shop
A complete unit of work	Each member of staff takes a product through the manufacturing process from beginning to end	A shop assistant offers advice to a customer, helps in trying on the clothes and then takes payment for the item
Direct feedback	Workers should check the quality of their own work, to provide feedback on whether they have done it effectively	The customer's reactions to the shop assistant will provide feedback on how well he has done his job
Direct communication	A worker finding a faulty component can go directly to the storage area to get a replacement without needing to check with a supervisor	The assistant can phone the warehouse to check whether or not that particular size can be ordered for the customer, without needing to consult with the manager

Financial reward systems

All the theorists agree that money is an important factor to consider in the performance of staff. A number of payment methods have been developed that try to use the power of financial reward to stimulate staff to work harder:

Financial reward system	What is it?	Advantages	Disadvantages
Piece work	Paying workers a fee for every unit of output completed. It is used most commonly on a production line	Encourages a fast rate of production by rewarding those workers that achieve the highest output	Can lead to poor quality of output as work is rushed. Makes workers less willing to accept changes to working practices, since they are likely to be slower at a new process
Performance related pay (PRP)	PRP links pay to an assessment of the employee's job performance	Rewards good job performance, judged according to pre-set criteria	Those who fail to 'make the grade' may be demotivated. May take up too much management time
Profit sharing	Workers are paid a bonus related to the amount of profit generated by the company or the site at which they work	Should encourage workers to work in a way that maximises profit, e.g. increasing productivity or reducing defect rates	May encourage a short-term approach to solving problems in order to protect this month's profit bonus
Share ownership	Involves issuing shares in the company to the workforce as part of their remuneration package	Ties the objectives of the workforce to shareholder objectives	Workers may feel that the total value of the shares they receive is insignificant
Fringe benefits	Non-financial rewards that can be given to staff, such as a company car or private health care	Can help meet employees' security needs, while some fringe benefits may go untaxed	Workers may prefer an increased pay packet that allows them to spend their money as they choose

Themes for evaluation

Is it real or just an illusion?

Take empowerment as an example. Many firms will happily use the term to describe how they treat their staff, but there is a genuine difference between empowering a worker and simply piling more jobs on their shoulders. Many of the motivational techniques suggested above have failed when put into practice simply because firms paid lip service to the ideas without ever fully committing to the cultural change required to make ideas such as empowerment provide the expected benefits.

Key Terms

Direct feedback – when the employee receives a response directly as a result of what they have done. A footballer gets the crowd's oohs or groans; a shopworker might get it from seeing a delighted bride-to-be trying on a beautiful dress.
Empowerment – when staff receive not only the power to decide how to do something (delegation) but also to decide what they should be doing.
Job enrichment – increasing employees' range of activities and responsibilities.

Test yourself

1 Identify three features of an 'enriched' job. (3)
2 Briefly explain two reasons why an advertising agency might benefit from moving towards a more team-based system. (4)
3 Explain the business significance of organisational culture. (5)
4 Explain two reasons why empowerment may not be an effective motivational tool for summer farm workers. (4)
5 Identify (explaining your reasons) the financial reward system that might work best for:
   a) sales staff in a fashion clothing shop
   b) the manager of a branch of a chain of fashion clothing retailers. (4)

Unit 27 Integrated people

AQA Business Studies for AS Revision Guide

The key issue is maximising the return from investing time, effort and resources into the people you employ. The investment can be measured in terms of the results from effective recruitment, training, motivation and organisation of staff.

Why?

People management is critical to the success of a business. Just as a manager would be angry at a machine that operated at only half its capabilities, so s/he should be unhappy if staff are operating at half their potential level of performance.

How much can they give?

This depends on how much you let them do, how much they can do and how you treat them. Some managers assume workers have little to offer and therefore ask for little. The result is that they tend to get as little as they expected. According to Professor Herzberg, well-designed jobs can allow staff to achieve, be creative and take some genuine control over their working lives. This will lead to staff who give all they can, instead of giving as little as they can get away with. Motivated staff will come up with good ideas and put them into practice with enthusiasm.

How do you get the most out of them?

- *Get the right people in at the right time with the right skills* – successful recruitment, selection and training of staff are vital. It is then important to organise staff in the right way, making it important to consider the organisation's structure.
- *Get them fired up and wanting the firm to succeed* – theorists can tell us the psychology of what motivates people, but putting that into practice is a tricky job for managers. With the need to keep staffing costs within budget, motivational techniques must pay for themselves.
- *Watch carefully for problems, using the methods for measuring workforce performance* – some managers will use these measures almost as a stick to beat their staff with, complaining that productivity is too low; other managers may see the measures as indicators of where there may be problems among the workforce that need to be investigated and solved.

Themes for evaluation

Straightforward knowledge and application of the theoretical aspects of people management should allow you to explain how firms could achieve better performance from the workforce. Beware, though, of all-purpose, simplistic answers. Managing people is difficult (ask the management of British Airways). Therefore answers should show an appreciation that different circumstances require different approaches. There are no magic solutions. Good people management is difficult and quite rare.

Test yourself

1. Outline two reasons for using a flat organisational structure. (4)
2. Briefly explain the relationship between spans of control and the height of an organisational structure. (3)
3. Outline one benefit and one drawback of internal recruitment. (4)
4. Which of the following job roles is likely to have the most authority and the least authority: Manager, Director, Team Leader. (2)
5. Explain the term delegation. (3)
6. Briefly explain F. W. Taylor's approach to paying staff. (3)
7. Outline one reason why a firm may choose to use on the job training instead of off the job training. (3)
8. What steps can a company take to meet employees' social needs? (4)
9. Distinguish between recruitment and selection. (3)
10. Explain what will occur, according to Herzberg, if an employee's hygiene needs are met. (3)
11. Using a motivation theory, explain why teamworking may help to motivate staff. (4)
12. List four financial incentives that may be offered to employees to encourage them to work harder. (4)
13. State the formula for calculating labour turnover. (2)
14. Explain one possible consequence of falling levels of labour productivity. (3)
15. Explain one possible cause of falling levels of labour productivity. (3)

Exam insight

Beware of overusing motivation theory. Every question you are asked is a specific question that needs a directly related answer – don't assume that all 'people' questions boil down to motivation theory. Exam questions on effective workforces tend (wrongly) to be answered purely in terms of motivation – don't ignore recruitment, selection, training and organisational structures.

Now try the following data response questions.

Data response: SCC Ltd

Simpson and Corteen Childcare (SCC) Ltd provided Britain's first nationwide babysitting service. From small beginnings, the company grew gradually to cover all of the UK's major cities. From a central call centre, customers can request babysitters with as little as one hour's notice and be sure that well-trained, police-checked staff will look after their children.

Careful people management allows the firm to recruit, train and check local staff before declaring the service available in each new location. The firm has a recruiting officer in each UK county responsible for visiting and organising training for new babysitters.

Nevertheless, much of the firm's operations are still controlled from Head Office by its founders Charlotte Simpson and Lydia Corteen. They feel that this level of control is crucial to ensure that all police checks are thoroughly handled and that customer service levels are maintained at the highest standards.

The firm now plans to diversify into dog-walking services. Simpson and Corteen are setting up a separate division under a new divisional manager to avoid overextending the founders' span of control.

Questions (allow 30 minutes)

1 Explain the term span of control. (3)
2 Outline the benefits that SCC Ltd experienced as a result of careful recruitment, selection and training. (6)
3 Analyse the reasons why the firm may have decided to use internal rather than external training. (7)
4 To what extent would SCC Ltd benefit from the use of more delegation? (9)

Data response: Ramsbottom Engineering

Jackie Jones runs a small company called Ramsbottom Engineering. It produces specialised industrial equipment. In the eight years she has been in charge, Jackie has introduced sweeping changes to the way in which the firm is run, having taken over from Tom, the son of the company's founder. When Tom's father ran the firm, a tall organisational structure was used, with staff being given very little freedom while supervisors were appointed to keep an eye on production staff. Jackie's arrival prompted a major shake-up, as she took all four supervisory staff away on a training weekend designed to encourage them to delegate more.

Within a few months of Jackie taking charge, the workforce had been empowered and Jackie's introduction of teamworking a year later proved a great success. With a surprisingly small number of staff leaving the firm (just 5 out of the 80 staff in a year), Jackie had managed to hold on to what she perceived to be their key asset – a vastly experienced and highly skilled staff. A further change was the introduction of profit sharing for all staff, a move welcomed by shop floor staff and supervisors alike.

Unfortunately, tough trading conditions led to a significant downturn in industrial investment. Work for the firm started to dry up. Jackie reached the point where she called her supervisors together to discuss the most likely candidates for what seemed to be the unavoidable round of redundancies. One supervisor suggested that they share the details of their problems with the shop floor staff to see whether they were able to come up with any solutions. Desperate to avoid making compulsory redundancies Jackie agreed, despite worrying about how the harsh reality of the firm's prospects might affect the morale of the workforce.

Questions (allow 30 minutes)

1 Calculate the firm's labour turnover in the year after Jackie took over. (3)
2 Analyse one benefit that Ramsbottom Engineering may have gained as a result of empowering its shop floor staff. (6)
3 Explain why Jackie was fearful of sharing the harsh truth with her staff. (6)
4 To what extent is Jackie's approach transferable to all companies? (10)

6 Operations management

Unit 28 Customer service

What?

Customer service is the term used to describe the different actions taken by a business when dealing with customers before, during and after purchase. Customer service is good when it meets or beats **customer expectations**. Passengers on a low-cost easyJet flight may be happier with the customer service than those on a British Airways flight, even though the absolute level of service on the British Airways flight was higher. The higher the expectations, the harder an organisation has to work at meeting them. At the time of writing, President Obama faces the equivalent problem in America. Voters expected so much from him that it will be hard for them not to be disappointed.

How?

Contact with customers may take place:
- by phone;
- on the internet;
- face to face.

Whichever medium is used by the firm to contact its customers, several key building blocks are needed to ensure they get customer service right.

- Identify exactly what level of service customers expect.
- Design a system (website, call centre script or guidelines for staff in-store) that will meet expectations.
- Train staff how to use the system and why it's important.
- Monitor the effectiveness of the customer service.

Why?

The three points listed below show the benefits to a business of effective customer service. In an exam, you will choose the benefits that best fit the business in the case study and tailor your explanation to suit that context.

Brand loyalty

Good customer service makes happy customers who are more than likely to come back to use the business they have enjoyed using next time they are going to make a purchase. A loyal customer base is created who will probably be receptive to new offerings from the business.

Stages in developing excellent customer service	Methods for achieving each stage
Identify exactly what customers expect	Market research is likely to be the key to identifying what customers actually want from the business. Unresearched assumptions as to what customers want may lead to one of two undesirable outcomes: substandard levels of service or expensive systems that customers don't want (and certainly don't want to pay for).
Design a system that will meet expectations	Most customers want to find out what they need quickly, with as little button-pressing or clicking as possible. This may require a business to hire a consultant who specialises in customer service systems. But the business itself must make sure that customers find the system pleasant to use.
Train staff	The HR department will probably be responsible for organising staff training, even if the training is led by customer service specialists.
Monitor the effectiveness of customer service	Checking or assuring quality may involve the use of mystery shoppers or recorded telephone calls from customers (quality control). Or the firm may rely on the success of the systems designed in the first place to ensure poor service cannot happen (quality assurance).

Word-of-mouth promotion

Happy customers may tell their friends about good customer service. A business with really good customer service turns its customers into **brand ambassadors** – keen to share their good experience with friends and family. This provides promotion free of charge.

Increased efficiency

With reduced product return levels and more happy customers with the right products sold to them, there will be far fewer administrative costs caused by products being returned and the need to calm down upset customers whose needs were not identified or appropriately met.

Themes for evaluation

Real or hype?

Firms that promise high levels of service must deliver, otherwise word of mouth will work against them as consumers are disappointed. In order for excellent customer service to happen, staff must be well-trained and motivated – otherwise the firm's promises may just be hype.

How important is customer service for this business?

All businesses will benefit from meeting or exceeding customer expectations of the level of service provided, but some may find their customers have low expectations. Just how much product knowledge do you expect shop assistants in a 'Pound Shop' to have? Saving money by only offering very basic levels of customer service may allow a firm to use those savings elsewhere – perhaps passing them on to customers in lower prices. In the case of a 'Pound Shop' this may be the very basis of their business model.

Exam conclusions?

Assess carefully the level of customer expectations for the firm in question before passing judgement on whether they need to improve their customer service. Do not simply assume that more customer service is always the right answer.

Application

Service business or manufacturing

Some features of customer service may only be found in the manufacturing sector – a physical product may carry a guarantee or warranty in case the product goes wrong. A haircut or insurance policy would offer no such guarantees. However, service sector businesses such as retailing are far more likely to have staff dealing directly with customers. So the immediate, face to face contact is a significant part of the quality of service they offer.

Key Terms

Brand ambassadors – customers who so love your product/service that they can't stop telling others – fantastic unpaid salespeople.

Customer expectations – what people expect when they experience buying and using a product or service; the higher the expectations, the harder it is to fulfil them.

Mystery shopper – someone hired to anonymously test customer service and then report back to senior management.

Exam insight

Exam questions may require an analysis of the possible benefits of providing excellent customer service. Such questions offer you a great chance to pick up analysis marks, since brand loyalty, word of mouth promotion and increased efficiency all have further knock-on effects that can be considered as part of a chain of logic. For example, you might need to explain how a hairdresser can benefit from better customer service. The chain of logic might include:- brand loyalty, allowing prices to be increased and therefore profit margins to rise. Or analyse how loyal customers are more likely to be regular users leading to a predictable and stable cash flow for the firm, even in difficult economic conditions.

Test yourself

1. Define 'good customer service'. (2)
2. Identify four actions that must be taken when making decisions on customer service within a business. (4)
3. Analyse two benefits to a high fashion clothing retailer of providing outstanding levels of customer service. (6)
4. State two businesses (excluding low cost airlines or Pound Shops) that may perform well with low levels of customer service. (2)
5. Analyse two possible causes of poor customer service. (6)

Unit 29 Effective quality management

What?

Quality management prevents defects, controls costs and generates customer satisfaction. It provides what the customer wants at the right time with the right level of quality and consistency.

Quality is hard to define. People do not always want the highest quality – sometimes cheap and cheerful is right. A golf beginner should buy lots of cheap, low-quality golf balls because they will get lost very quickly.

Another definition is 'fit for use'. For some products quality is defined by law. The law lays down minimum quality standards. This particularly applies to products where health or safety is involved. Food must be fresh and has to be handled in certain ways. It is illegal to sell electrical equipment without a plug fitted.

Who?

Quality is important for all firms. In a competitive market it will be more significant. In industrial markets (business to business) firms will often define minimum standards for their suppliers. This helps them to maintain their own quality standards. Large businesses such as supermarkets and chain stores are able to insist on quality standards. They have the buying power to force their suppliers to conform. They may insist that their suppliers have obtained ISO 9000, which is an internationally recognised quality accreditation.

Some large industries have watchdogs that ensure that minimum standards are met. OFWAT (the water industry regulator) has the task of ensuring that water quality is maintained.

For all businesses there is no doubt that customers have perception of quality and use it as part of the buying decision making process. Having a quality image is one of the main ingredients for a good brand image.

Why?

Quality is an important competitive issue. Its importance will depend on how competitive the market is. A good quality product will:
- be easier to establish in the market;
- generate repeat purchases and therefore a longer life cycle;

- allow brand building and cross-marketing;
- allow a price premium.

Quality problems will have cost implications for the firm. These include:
- loss of sales;
- scrapping of unsuitable goods;
- loss of reputation;
- reworking of unsatisfactory goods – costs of labour and materials;
- may have to price discount;
- lower prices for 'seconds';
- may impact on other products in range;
- handling complaints/warranty claims;
- retailers may be unwilling to stock goods;
- loss of consumer goodwill and repeat purchases.

Exam insight

When answering questions about quality management, think beyond the production department. Quality issues are often closely interwoven with other parts of the business. Links with motivation theory and the role of the employee in quality control are important issues.

When suggesting quality initiatives or solutions to quality problems, remember to consider not only how the initiatives work but also the problems that they may cause.

How?

The ideal is to detect quality problems before they reach the customer. Most quality control processes are concentrated in the factory. These aim to prevent faults leaving the factory. This can be done by:
- inspection of finished goods before sale – this may be all goods or only a sample;
- self-inspection of work by operatives – this is being used more as businesses recognise that quality needs to be 'everyone's business';
- statistical analysis within the production process – this can be used to ensure that specifications stay within certain limits.

A good quality management system will have four stages of quality control: prevention, detection, correction and improvement.
- Prevention: to try to avoid problems occurring, for example at the design stage.
- Detection: ensuring that quality problems are spotted before they reach the customer.

- Correction: this is not just about correcting faults it is also about discovering why there is a problem.
- Improvement: customer expectations of quality are always changing.

Quality initiatives

As the importance of quality has been recognised there has been a growth in initiatives to control and improve quality.

- *Total quality management* – This is a way of looking at quality issues whereby every employee and every part of the business takes responsibility for quality control and improvement.
- *Training* – This can make an enormous contribution to quality. It might be specifically job orientated such as training a machinist, or a sales assistant in customer care. It is important where the company is trying to introduce a 'quality culture'.
- *Quality assurance* – Schemes such as ISO 9000 provide customers with confidence that a supplier has a documented quality system operating throughout the company and involving suppliers and subcontractors.
- *Continuous improvement* – This is a system where the whole organisation is committed to making changes on a continual basis. The Japanese call it *kaizen*.
- *Zero defects* – The aim is to produce goods and services with no faults or problems. It is a *management philosophy* and requires commitment throughout the organisation. It emphasises that each employee must contribute to quality.
- *Quality circles* – This is a group of employees who meet together for the purpose of identifying problems and recommending adjustments to the working processes.
- *Benchmarking* – This is a process of comparing a business with other businesses. Having identified the best, businesses attempt to bring their performance up to the level of the best, by adopting its practices.

Key Terms

Competitiveness – the ability of a firm to be better than its competitors

Continuous improvement – a management philosophy that encourages everyone in the business to look for ways of making improvements to the company's efficiency

ISO 9000 – an internationally recognised quality assurance certificate; firms have to show that they have quality maintenance processes, which are documented and inspected

Total quality management – a management philosophy that insists that quality is the responsibility of everyone in the organisation

But

Quality initiatives may be expensive. It is possible to get 100 per cent quality at a cost. It is necessary to balance the cost of quality control and improvement with the costs of poor quality. The company needs to be aware of how much the customer is prepared to pay.

Application

Mattel, the world's largest toy maker, had a quality disaster in 2007. It was forced to withdraw millions of toys from the market. They estimated that this would cost them over £15 million. This did not take into account any long-term damage that might result from customers losing confidence in the company and its products.

The reasons for the recall was that toys made in China were found to have unacceptable levels of lead in the paint and others had loose parts that could be a danger to children. This story highlights the difficulty of controlling quality when large businesses outsource manufacturing. The response from the business was to implement plans for additional checking and to reduce outsourcing by shifting production to its own factories away from subcontractors. The company is hoping that these moves will restore public confidence in the products.

Themes for evaluation

Often quality initiatives require a long-term view. There may be a conflict between short-term costs and longer-term results. Shareholders may want returns today but the benefits may take some time to show.

Increased quality brings its own rewards in the marketplace. Companies have also found that the initiatives, especially where they are people-based, have also brought other advantages. Changes in working practices have improved motivation and efficiency and have reduced waste and costs.

Test yourself

1 What is meant by quality management? (2)
2 Give two reasons why quality management is important. (4)
3 Explain two ways to control quality in a factory. (4)
4 What management initiatives contribute to quality management? (4)
5 Outline two costs that are incurred as a result of quality problems. (4)
6 What is the right level of quality? (8)

Unit 30 Working with suppliers

What?

A supplier is any organisation that provides another business with products or services used in running that business. This will include the supplier of raw materials or components to a manufacturer; in addition, most firms will need suppliers of electricity, equipment or **outsourced** services such as staff training.

Many businesses have suppliers that they depend on. In 2009, with car factories closed across Europe and America, several car producers provided finance to key suppliers that would have collapsed without financial support. Although some suppliers may be critical, many others provide products or services that are offered by many rival firms. In this case, the purchaser is in a great position to negotiate toughly, and therefore minimise the variable costs of production.

How to choose the right supplier

Several factors are likely to affect any choice of supplier. These factors should be learned:

Why work closely with suppliers?

There are several benefits to forging a long-lasting relationship with suppliers.

- *Working together to develop new products* – designing complex new products, such as cars, can be helped immensely by working with suppliers in order to assess in the early stages of the design process just what suppliers will be able to offer, perhaps when considering a new design of heated car seat.
- *Flexibility* – a supplier will be more willing to help out in times of difficulty if they see their customer as being a valuable long-term client. Where supplies of a product, such as a new games console, are limited, manufacturers are likely to supply retailers with whom they have had a consistently good relationship over the long term. Alternatively, a restaurant that is running desperately short of burger buns may find its supplier is willing to make a special delivery to prevent them running out before tomorrow's scheduled delivery.
- *Improved efficiency* – sharing information on when supplies are needed will help suppliers to ensure that you get just what you need when you need it,

Factor affecting choice of supplier	Explanation	Especially important when
Cost	Perhaps the most obvious method of comparing suppliers	A firm has very low profit margins or the item supplied accounts for a large proportion of their total costs
Quality	Poor quality items are likely to cause problems as equipment can fail or faulty products are made with poor materials	A firm's reputation is built on the quality of its products or service
Reliability	If suppliers deliver late then production may grind to a halt, leaving the firm paying for staff and materials not producing	A firm is operating with very little stock such as those using a **just-in-time** system
Frequency	Daily deliveries allow firms to minimise the amount of stock they have to keep – thus reducing their costs	Stock-holding space is limited, supplies are perishable or a just-in-time system is being used
Flexibility	Some suppliers will only be able to deliver at set times, however, others may be willing to make a delivery when you need it	Demand is unpredictable
Payment terms	The ability to buy on credit offers advantages to a firm's cash flow, since delaying the outflow for paying suppliers allows the firm to hang on to its cash for longer	A firm is experiencing cash flow problems

the classic case of this being a major supermarket whose tills are linked to the production planning software at their supplier's factory automatically telling the supplier when the supermarket needs extra stocks of baked beans or bread.

Each of these benefits invites you to develop a line of argument that considers the knock-on impact of the benefits occurring.

Application

The third column in the table above should give you hints as to what to look for when seeking to gain application marks on a question about suppliers. Identifying what type of firm you are dealing with in your case study will help you to pick which features of a supplier are most important, so a firm that is known to be experiencing cash flow problems may choose a supplier that offers generous credit terms, even if they are not the cheapest. Meanwhile, firms with a reputation for quality, such as Thornton's chocolates, may well choose a supplier that offers high quality, even if other factors, such as the price, are not the best on offer.

Exam insight

Many students get caught out trying to list as many different points as they can remember. You should never find yourself trying to cover all the factors affecting the choice of supplier in an answer. Look for the clues in case study as to what is particularly important for this firm and discuss the two or three most important factors for this firm.

Themes for evaluation

The most likely evaluative question on this topic will invite you to decide which supplier a firm should use. Assessing the different factors that might help a firm to decide will be necessary, before deciding on which factors are most important for the business. This will form the basis of a sound piece of judgement rooted in the context of the case study. Note that the correct judgement will require you to decide on the most important factor. To justify this, it is important to consider other factors and thereby provide some balance in your response.

Key Terms

Just-in-time – operating with virtually zero buffer stock, and therefore relying hugely on the efficiency and reliability of your suppliers

Outsourced (also outsourcing) getting an external business to supply part of the way your business operates, for example IT services

Test yourself

1 Identify three factors other than price and quality that will affect the choice of supplier for a car manufacturer. (3)

2 Analyse two benefits of Primark developing a long-term relationship with the manufacturers it uses to produce its clothing. (6)

3 Briefly explain why reliability is an important factor for a restaurant to consider when choosing a food supplier. (3)

4 Analyse one benefit to Tesco of choosing a supplier of bananas that is willing to offer two weeks' credit. (3)

Unit 31 Capacity utilisation

What?

Capacity utilisation measures how much of a firm's capacity is actually being used. A half-full Wembley means the stadium has a capacity utilisation of 50 per cent. Capacity utilisation is calculated by taking current output as a percentage of maximum possible output:

$$\frac{\text{current output}}{\text{maximum output}} \times 100$$

Why is it important?

The single most important concept related to capacity utilisation is that of fixed cost per unit. The closer a firm gets to its maximum capacity utilisation (100 per cent), the lower the amount of fixed costs carried by each unit of output. Fixed costs in total stay the same from 0 to maximum output, so the more units of output they are spread across, the lower the fixed costs carried by each unit and the greater the profit per unit.

Application

To return to the Wembley stadium example, a Rock Promoter would have to pay £200,000 a night to hire the stadium. On top, there would be fixed costs (security staff and so on) of £80,000. If 14,000 come to the event, the fixed costs per customer would be £280,000/14,000 = £20. Whereas if 28,000 come, the fixed costs per person slip to £280,000/28,000 = £10. In a stadium that can hold 50,000, the higher the capacity utilisation, the lower the fixed costs per customer. And therefore the higher the profit per customer.

What?

The ideal capacity utilisation should be 100 per cent. This allows the firm to minimise fixed costs per unit and therefore maximise profit. Though this logic is sound, few firms can safely operate at 100 per cent capacity utilisation for any length of time. This is because there would be no time available to carry out routine maintenance tasks. In reality, most firms like to operate at 90–95 per cent of capacity.

How?

There are two ways to increase capacity utilisation: increase current output or reduce maximum capacity.

Increase current output

Increasing current output will spread fixed costs over more units and therefore achieve the objective behind increasing capacity utilisation. However, there is little point in increasing output unless you can sell the extra items you are producing. It is vital to consider how you will sell those extra items. If extra sales are the result of a price cut, have you actually reduced your price by more than your fixed costs per unit have fallen?

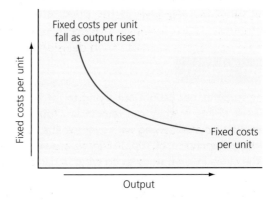

Fig. 31A: Falling fixed costs per unit

Reduce maximum capacity

Reducing maximum capacity will also have the desired effect of reducing fixed costs per unit by reducing your total fixed costs. Laying off staff, closing down an under-used factory, or moving to smaller premises will allow a firm to reduce its total fixed costs. Therefore, with an unchanged output, fixed costs per unit will be lower as there are fewer fixed costs to be covered.

Why may utilisation be low?

Business	Cause
At a leisure centre	Demand is high after work in the evenings, but low during the working day

Business	Cause
At a third division football club	The ground was built when larger crowds were common, perhaps when the club was doing better
Producing Cadbury's Creme Eggs	Production is flat out from the autumn through to Easter, but halted between Easter and the late summer

Which is the best choice?

The solution to a problem of low capacity utilisation should be appropriate to the causes of the problem.

If the causes of the capacity utilisation problem are short term (such as a seasonal dip in sales), a short-term solution should be found. This will usually involve marketing activities such as price discounting.

Cutting capacity will be a longer-term answer to a longer-term problem. If a market has declined and the firm feels unable to reinvigorate sales in that market, it may decide to reduce capacity. It may lay off staff or even close down a production line or a whole factory. These actions are hard to reverse so the firm is unlikely to rush into such decisions.

What next?

Flexibility is crucial in coping with low levels of capacity use. If the company is able to identify a core of key staff and assets that will allow it to function at a low level of output while keeping fixed costs low, they know they have a 'fall back' position when demand is low and output needs to be low. Extra production, when required, can be added through the use of temporary staff, rented machinery and premises, or even through the use of subcontracting. In this way, a firm would be able to operate at a high level of capacity utilisation even when demand is low, while retaining the flexibility to increase output when the need arises.

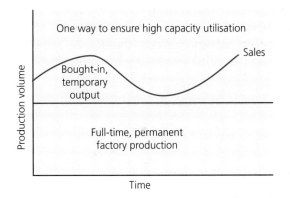

Fig. 31B: The value of flexibility

Themes for evaluation

How big a problem is it?

A firm with low capacity utilisation may not have a particularly big problem. In some cases firms will expect a low level of capacity utilisation during certain periods of the year. They may have already taken steps to cope with this, by using quiet periods to train staff or update machinery and equipment. Although fixed costs per unit will be high during these periods, the firm may benefit from higher quality standards in the medium term.

Is the capacity utilisation the cause or effect of the problem?

Low levels of capacity utilisation cause higher costs per unit and therefore may tempt firms to charge higher prices. This may be the reason why demand for the product is low, so low capacity utilisation is the cause of the problem. Alternatively, the weak demand could be the effect of external factors such as the arrival of a new competitor. This would mean that the low level of capacity utilisation is simply an indicator of a problem elsewhere.

Key Terms

Capacity – the amount of units of output that can be created by a firm in a given period of time (also referred to as maximum capacity)
Fixed costs per unit – spreading total fixed costs over the number of sales you make; the higher the sales, the more thinly the fixed costs are spread
Subcontracting – getting another factory to produce your goods for you, to your exact requirements

Test yourself

1. What is the current level of capacity utilisation for a firm with a maximum output of 25,000 units per month that is currently making 20,000 units? (2)
2. If the firm's fixed costs per month are £100,000, what are fixed costs per unit at:
   a) their current output? (3)
   b) 100 per cent capacity utilisation? (3)
3. Briefly explain how you could see that capacity utilisation was low at:
   a) a manufacturing plant (3)
   b) a hotel (3)
4. Outline two actions that could be taken to increase capacity utilisation at a leisure centre. (6)

Unit 32 Making operational decisions

What?

Operations management is the process of ensuring that customers receive what they want, when and where they want it. It is the business function that provides the supply to meet the demand from the consumer.

The key operational decisions on which you may be tested concern:
- matching production to demand;
- operational targets;
- capacity utilisation;
- non-standard orders.

Why?

Successful operations management relies on sensible decision-making by directors and managers with responsibility for the production of goods and provision of services. The most basic operational decision is how much of a product or service to make in any given time period.

Matching production to demand

Failing to produce enough products to meet demand from customers or retailers leads to lost revenue and damages the firm's reputation for reliability. In a service business such as a car servicing garage, insufficient staffing or equipment might mean losing customers to rival firms. Even the most loyal are unlikely to wait several weeks to have their car serviced.

On the other hand, making more than can be sold may lead to such high stock levels that some products must simply be thrown away. In a service business such as a hairdresser, having too many staff available means paying people to sit around who are unable to generate revenue for the business. Therefore, striking the right balance between making too much or too little is critical for a business.

Application

In 2008, shoemaker Crocs increased production, anticipating another year of sales growth. Unfortunately the shoes started to drift out of fashion, leaving the business with huge stocks and a bit of a cash flow problem. It was forced to throw away $70 million of shoes and write them off in its accounts. Overproduction is an expensive mistake.

Making an accurate sales forecast will form the basis of the decisions required when planning production levels:
- how many staff are needed;
- how much equipment and space are needed;
- how much stock to order.

However, sales forecasting is tricky, given how many different factors, many highly unpredictable, can affect demand. Managers able to make consistently accurate sales forecasts will be highly valued staff members.

Some simple guidelines are shown below for decision-making:

Plan to produce slightly more than you may need	Try to ensure production never exceeds demand
If the product can be kept in stock without losing value, e.g. furniture makers	Where stocks are perishable or highly fashion-driven
If the product is subject to sudden surges in demand due to external factors such as temperature	Where the costs of maintaining excess capacity are high, for example employing very highly skilled staff
You have many close competitors to whom customers may switch if you cannot meet demand	If you have a unique product that customers will be willing to wait for

Whenever making production decisions it is important to remember that:
- Increasing production will hurt (short-term) cash flow.
- Increasing production requires careful coordination with other departments, such as Human Resources (do we need to hire more staff?), Marketing (is there enough demand?) and Finance (do we need to raise extra finance from the bank or from our shareholders?).

Key Terms

Capacity utilisation – the extent to which a firm's actual output uses its maximum possible output, for example a half-empty plane means a capacity utilisation of 50 per cent

Non-standard (special) order – a one-off order that might be accepted at discounted prices (perhaps to make use of under-utilised capacity)

Operational targets

Targets will be set within the operations management section of the firm. This will bring the following advantages:
- gives staff something to aim for;
- gives a morale boost if targets are achieved;
- helps the overall planning process of the business.

There are three main variables for which targets will be set.

Unit costs

Calculated by dividing total costs by output, the cost of making one unit of output is a critical factor for any firm. Reducing unit costs will enable a firm to choose between two attractive options:
- lower selling prices without losing profit;
- maintain selling prices but make the same profit per unit.

Though no firm can keep reducing unit costs forever, many firms will feature unit cost reduction as a key target due to the benefits this brings.

Capacity utilisation

High levels of capacity utilisation are needed in order to keep unit costs as low as possible. As a result, many firms will see capacity utilisation levels as a key variable for target setting. Airlines are especially keen to reach targets for the average percentage of seats filled and adjust prices on a regular basis to try to ensure that each flight hits its target for the percentage of seats filled.

Quality

For firms whose reputation is heavily reliant on quality, quality targets form a vital way to measure performance. Typical examples include the number of customer returns as a percentage of total sales and the percentage of customers who make complaints. Firms dealing with very expensive raw materials or components will be keen to set targets designed to minimise the waste produced by production mistakes. These mistakes are likely to make a serious dent in profits.

Non-standard orders

The final type of operational decision to cover is whether or not to accept non-standard orders from customers. The two typical types of non-standard order are:
- high-price special orders;
- low-price special orders.

High-price special orders occur when a customer wants something special from a business, whether it be adjustments to the product design or an unusually fast delivery time. Careful consideration of the possible extra costs will be needed to ensure that they are still below the special price offered.

Low-price special orders occur when a customer asks for a special price cut when buying from a business. For example: 'We usually buy 1000 widgets from you; can you give us a 20 per cent discount if we buy 5000 this time?' Special orders can still be profitable, most notably if the special order can be met simply by using existing spare capacity. In these cases, as long as the firm has already passed its break-even point, the cost of providing the order should be equal to the extra variable costs involved, since no extra fixed costs should arise.

Themes for evaluation

You may be asked to make an operational decision based on the information provided in your exam case study. Weigh up the two sides to the decision, for example accept/don't accept the order. Though you may not feel confident about 'the right answer', remember that real managers in real businesses face the same hurdle as you. They may be worried that a wrong decision could be costly. Luckily for you, the examiner does not have a fixed idea of 'the right answer'. He or she will accept your ideas, as long as you explain your reasoning.

Exam insight

The topic of operational targets gives examiners a chance to test your ability to make judgements in context by asking you which types of targets are likely to be most important for the firm in your case study. Good answers will consider the relative importance of any of the three types of target mentioned. Then move on to decide which is likely to be most important for that particular firm. Look for hints in the case study, such as:
- firms selling products cheaply will have to focus on unit costs;
- those selling at higher prices may need to focus on quality targets;
- firms with high fixed costs (such as airlines) will want to ensure capacity utilisation targets are met.

Test yourself

1. Outline two possible problems for a bakery of failing to produce enough bread to meet demand. (4)
2. Analyse one problem for Primark of ordering more flip-flops than customers want to buy. (5)
3. Explain one reason why a winemaker may decide not to shut down and sell off one of its bottling plants despite very low levels of capacity utilisation during a recession. (3)
4. Identify three possible reasons why a farmer may agree to sell 20,000 chickens to Tesco for a lower price than the farmer usually charges. (3)
5. Analyse the possible benefits of setting clear operational targets for a business. (5)

Unit 33 Using technology in operations

What?

This topic concerns the various ways that modern companies are using computer technology to control operations.

How?

- *Automated stock control* – bar codes are used in conjunction with checkouts or a bar code reader on the production line to monitor which items of stock have been used up or sold, allowing automatic reordering at suppliers.
- *Design* – computer aided design (CAD) allows much of the design process to be carried out on computer simulations, eliminating the need for expensive prototype building and testing.
- *Robotics* – machines that can be programmed to perform a repetitive task over and over again. Robots can also complete tasks that are bad for human health, such as spending eight hours every day spraying paint on cars. Robots can bring a higher degree of accuracy as well as reducing the need for staff and the costs of employing those staff. Despite all these advantages, industrial robots have not become as widespread as people expected; humans remain highly effective competitors!
- *Communication with customers* – a company website can be used not just to provide information, but also as a place to buy. Some firms only sell their products via their websites, whilst others, notably in the travel industry, make the majority of their sales through their websites. In addition, technology can be used to build a database of customers in order to gather a detailed picture of the people who use your business. Supermarket loyalty cards, such as Tesco's Clubcard, store data on customers so that mailings about special offers can be targeted at customers most likely to be interested in the deals.
- *Communication with suppliers* – technology offers the opportunity to automate communication with suppliers. Networked links between a firm and its suppliers brings improved speed, accuracy and detail to communication. This allows a stronger relationship to be built, as well as a far smoother service being provided by suppliers. This, in turn, makes it possible to run precise systems such as just-in-time stock ordering.

Why?

Four major benefits of using technology in operations are shown in the first column of the table below. The role of each form of technology is explained on the right.

	Automated stock control	Design	Robotics	Communication with customers	Communication with suppliers
Reducing costs	Accurate stock control should avoid carrying excess stocks which may become unusable	CAD should reduce design costs as fewer prototypes need to be made; computer testing may be hugely cheaper than in the real world	The ability to shed staff reduces the ongoing wage bill of the organisation	The use of databases to target promotional activity helps to cut waste within the firm's marketing spending	Suppliers may have suggestions as to how the firm can reduce its costs relating to the products being supplied
Improving quality	With stocks always available, there should be no need to offer poor quality service or use substandard components in a manufacturing process	Well designed products are easier to make simply and likely to function better for consumers. Rigorous testing using CAD should help to ensure both of these benefits occur	Robots are likely to bring improved accuracy to operations, leading to fewer defects	Strong customer databases should ensure the firm can offer the products that best suit customers' needs, resulting in fewer product returns	Giving suppliers enough notice of when new stocks are needed should ensure better quality service for customers if the products they need are available

	Automated stock control	Design	Robotics	Communication with customers	Communication with suppliers
Reducing waste	For firms selling fresh produce or technological items, careful stock control cuts the number of items that must be sold off cheaply	Clever design, carefully worked through using CAD should be able to minimise the materials needed in the production of a product	Fewer quality defects will lead to less materials' wastage	Targeted customer databases reduce the 'junk mail' problem of people throwing away materials they do not want	EDI systems are the driving force behind the improved stock control that helps prevent the need to dispose of outdated stock
Improving productivity	Preventing production stoppages caused by running out of stocks of a particular part or component	Careful design and CAD testing of workspaces should reduce the distance staff need to move, thus speeding up production time	With no need for breaks or holidays, robots should boost productivity levels	Processing orders through a website will generally help to automate the order processing, thus speeding up this process	Automated stock ordering can ensure that deliveries arrive much quicker – preventing production stoppages

However

Cost

The initial purchase of a piece of technology is likely to be high. Funding such a large purchase may prove hard, although credit may be available to help spread the cost and relieve the cash flow problems.

Training

Staff that will operate the technology are likely to need to be trained in how to use the specific equipment purchased. This of course will carry a further cost burden.

Job fears

Often technology will be used to replace employees, prompting fears of redundancy for staff.

Exam insight

Application is again a critical factor when answering questions about technology. Good answers will point out which use of technology is most appropriate for the business given in the case study. An answer that explains which benefits are most likely to occur from the introduction of a given piece of technology will set you apart from students giving generic answers about 'all businesses' or 'all technology'.

Themes for evaluation

Always look to balance the benefits of using technology against the costs of buying, installing and running it. It is often easy to get carried away with the benefits of using technology while losing sight of the fact that much high-tech equipment carries a very high initial cost that a firm may not be able to afford. It is also important to remember that the future is not predictable. Some branches of Woolworths were being fitted with new, expensive check-out systems a few months before the whole chain closed down. What a waste of money.

Test yourself

1 Outline two benefits to Primark of using CAD. (4)
2 Explain why an EDI link with Sainsbury's is vital for a small smoothie manufacturer. (4)
3 Outline two reasons why a car manufacturer may gain a competitive advantage by investing heavily in production robots. (4)
4 Explain two benefits to McDonald's of automated stock control. (4)
5 Outline two benefits to an airline of only taking bookings online. (4)

Unit 34 Integrated operations management

The AQA specification for this unit says:

Candidates should understand how operations management can help a business to be more effective and the role that can be played in this by technology.

As you study the topics within operations management you should keep being struck by the importance of **efficiency** and how it interlinks with business **profitability**.

Remember: profit = revenue − costs

Capacity utilisation is important to minimise costs, thus enabling competitive pricing or enhanced profitability. Understanding economies and diseconomies of scale makes the business aware of costs and what it can do to minimise them. Cost savings obviously help profitability.

Improved profitability means that the business can grow and it has resources to invest in research and development or in better machinery or even staff training. Having lower costs also helps in the market place. If costs are lower, the business has more pricing options. It could also use some of the costs saved in production for other marketing initiatives such as advertising and branding.

Good quality contributes not only to the marketing effort but also improves profitability through savings on reworking and reduction in wastage. Initiatives such as Kaizen and lean production not only improve production efficiency but also contribute to motivating and empowering the workforce. Effective stock control improves cash flow and makes savings to variable costs and fixed overheads.

As you answer questions linked to operations management, try to see these topics in this wider context. If you are analysing a process improvement, try to consider what other effects it will have on the business:

● How are people affected?
● Does this contribute to the marketing effort? (Perhaps by producing a better quality product or by producing it cheaper so enabling the business to be more competitive.)
● How does it affect the finances of the business? (Perhaps by reducing costs or cash flow needs or increasing profitability.)

Throughout all of this look at how technology is helping firms to manage the business. Computerised production can reduce stock levels by allowing the introduction of a just-in-time system. Robot technology can reduce defects in the production process. Automated stock picking can speed up the distribution process and information technology has made a huge contribution to administration efficiency.

Remember to look at the whole picture as this will give you a firm base for evaluation.

Test yourself (50 marks)

1 What is meant by benchmarking? (3)
2 What is a quality circle and what does it contribute? (4)
3 How could a firm increase its capacity utilisation? (3)
4 Explain how economies of scale reduce unit costs. (2)
5 Why might diseconomies of scale occur? (2)
6 What is the difference between batch and job production? (3)
7 What problems might occur if the firm is using just-in-time stock control? (4)
8 What influences the minimum level of stock a business needs to maintain? (3)
9 How does quality management contribute to the marketing effort? (3)
10 Why do average costs generally fall when output is increased? (3)
11 Explain one way that new technology has helped business efficiency. (3)
12 Which sort of production process is most suitable for mass-produced goods and why? (4)
13 What is Kaizen and what is required for it to succeed? (4)
14 What is the principle behind total quality management? (2)
15 How does good stock control help to improve cash flow? (3)
16 What are the advantages and disadvantages of automating parts of the production process? (4)

Now try the following data response questions. Allow yourself 30 minutes for each one.

Data response: Online stock management

Internet-based stock management systems are now available to help local authorities manage their gritting programmes. The De-Icing Business, which supplies salt products to local authorities, has a web-based stock management system that allows local authorities and contractors to manage their stock of salt online.

De-Icing Business customers are able to access daily stock data and see exactly how much stock has been used at each depot. Online reporting allows customers to accurately monitor salt stocks and gritter performance to ensure that every penny of the winter salting budget works as hard as possible. The Wintranet uploads data from each salt storage location. The gritters drive over a weighbridge every time they leave and return to the depot. This enables the calculation of how much salt has been spread en-route. By comparing daily stock usage figures against agreed stock profiles the system can provide early warning of potential low stock and automatically generate an order to restock when necessary.

Another feature is the use of global positioning satellites to track the precise position of gritters, providing proof of the exact times and route on which salting occurred. As well as enabling accurate monitoring of gritter performance, this data is crucial for managers and local authorities in case of legal action from road users involved in accidents. These highly advanced features can improve control over the gritting operation to ensure that adequate service levels are delivered.

(Source: Adapted from The De-Icing Business website)

Questions

1 Why is it important for local authorities to maintain adequate stocks of salt? (2)
2 What advantages does an automated stock management system give? (4)
3 Consider the advantages and disadvantages of a computerised production process. (6)
4 In this case the system helps the business to deliver a quality service. Why is quality control important for businesses? (5)
5 Some businesses use a just-in-time system of stock management. Explain how this works and evaluate the pros and cons for a medium-sized business producing sandwiches for sale in supermarkets. (8)

Data response: Challenge 50

The Maruti car factory in India had set its workers and management a challenge: *Challenge 50* aims for a 50 per cent improvement in productivity and quality and a 30 per cent reduction in costs over 3 years. The first year of the challenge has shown remarkable results, as shown in the table below.

As a result of cost savings, Maruti has been able to reduce the price of its small car, the Maruti 800, to below the price in 2000. Consequently, sales have increased by over 30 per cent. This was not a forced price reduction and the forecast profit for this model was expected to stay the same. The company was hoping to take advantage of growing sales. This signals a change from the business being production led to being market led.

So how have Maruti managers achieved this?

● They have benchmarked against the 'best in class' Suzuki's Kosai plant in Japan. Among other things this has led to a redesign of the working area to reduce the number of steps taken to perform a task. As the chairman of Suzuki says, 'We pay people to work, not walk.'
● They have made changes in philosophy and application of the Kaizen system that has been operating for several years.

Man hours per vehicle index (base 1999–2000 = 100)	76	59
Ratio of stock to sales index (base 1999–2000 = 100)	59	41
Average defects per vehicle	60%	33%
Direct pass rate	20%	40%
Inspection workers per shift	8	2
Cars per day (output)	730	1,700
Employees	4,800	4,600
Kaizen suggestions	60,000	72,000
Number of suppliers	300	245

(Source: Extracted from Business Standard; India)

Questions

1 What is meant by the sentence: 'Both of these moves signal a change from the business being production led to being market led'? (2)
2 Explain briefly how the number of cars produced per day can increase when the number of employees is falling. (3)
3 Explain why the company has benchmarked against the Suzuki plant in Japan and the benefits of this process. (7)
4 The business is operating a Kaizen system. Evaluate some of the advantages and disadvantages of this. (9)

7 Marketing and the competitive environment

Unit 35 Introduction to effective marketing

What?

Marketing is the business activity that links the producer to the customer. Marketing is not just about advertising – it is about having the right product available to customers in the right place and at the right price. In addition the business must promote the product in the right way to achieve satisfactory sales.

Why?

Good marketing can enhance the image of the company and its products and so contribute to sales and profitability. Effective marketing is about using marketing activity to achieve the business objectives cost-effectively. A poorly targeted campaign is a waste of time and money.

How?

Identifying the target market

In order to make marketing activity effective the business needs to know who it is selling to. All businesses need to identify their *target market*. They need to know who the customers are and why they will buy the product. This clearly will be more difficult for a new product than an existing one.

One way of identifying the target market is to differentiate between the *mass market* (appealing to a large number of people) or a *niche market (a* specialised small part of the market) See Unit 36.

Even in a mass market not all consumers are the same and it is often helpful to break the market down into smaller units known as *market segments*. Firms such as SKY TV recognise that customers have different tastes and allow them to select packages that suit them.

There are many different ways of segmenting the market. These include:

- *Gender* – males and females have specific products targeted at them and methods of packaging may differ to appeal to one sex or the other. Look at bottles of shampoo or deodorants.
- *Spending power* – some products are specifically aimed at high-income spenders. Others at lower income groups. Look at the difference between Waitrose and Aldi.
- *Age* – products that appeal to younger people may be marketed differently from those aimed at a more mature market, for example. Nintendo games and Brain Trainer.

Market knowledge

Once the firm has identified its target market it needs to ensure that it understands how the market works. It needs to know the size of the market and the state of competition. Most importantly it needs to understand customer tastes, attitudes and behaviour. This should be easy for a small business with close day-to-day contact with its customers. The owner needs to know how customers will react to changes in the product or prices and, just as importantly, how competitors will react.

Having good market knowledge gives the firm the background in which to begin the process of selling to the customer. Market research is the key to gaining market knowledge and to planning effective marketing.

Key features of effective marketing

- *Market knowledge* – effective marketing starts with good market knowledge so that marketing activity can be focused on what the customer wants. This is known as market orientated marketing.
- *Value for money* – if marketing is to be efficient it needs to give value for money. The return should be greater than the cost. Firms need to know:
  - What does our marketing activity cost?
  - Can we afford it?
  - What do we get in return?
- *Working together* – the marketing function should not operate in isolation from the rest of the business. The whole of the company must work together if

marketing expenditure is to be effective. Finance is needed to fund a marketing programme and production and distribution must be ready to deal with any increases in sales. A marketing objective of increasing sales will only work if the production department can produce sufficient items.

Marketing is everyone's job

The most effective marketing activity is when everyone in the business is working towards the same goal of selling the best possible products or services in the most profitable way. Efficiency in production will mean less quality issues and lower costs. Good customer service will make the product easier to sell and enhance the brand image. Efficient distribution will make sure that the product is available when and where it is needed.

Application

In July 2009 the Cambridge Catering and Cleaning Services (CCS) won an award for their marketing campaign to get more children to eat school meals. Following Jamie Oliver's campaign for better school meals many parents stopped their children having school dinners. The result was a £1 million deficit for the service. Using a marketing firm they launched a turnaround programme aimed at increasing meal numbers to at least 200,000, which would enable them to break even.

Firstly they carried out market research talking to parents, pupils, catering staff and head teachers. Following this they had a several-pronged approach that included:

- A marketing training programme for school caterers to enable them to run their own promotions.
- Informing parents about menus through leaflets and their website and through menu boards in primary schools.
- A conference for catering staff where they explained the results of the market research.

The results were impressive: over 200,000 meals will be served in the financial year and the service is likely to break even. One of the judges was impressed by the way they involved all the interested parties and based their campaign on feedback from good research.

Themes for evaluation

Is the amount of money spent on marketing worthwhile?

There is an argument which says that consumers would be better served if businesses spent less on marketing and more on improving the product or service and reducing prices to customers. In defence, marketing experts would say that marketing means that the customer is aware of the product and is also aware of competitive products so is in a better position to make a choice.

Is marketing ethical?

There are many people who think that persuading customers to buy products is unethical, particularly when targeted at vulnerable groups (for example, positioning sweets at supermarket checkout tills or persuading customers in developing countries to buy cigarettes). The firms would argue that the justification for trying to sell their products is that this is necessary to keep staff in a job and provide a return to their shareholders. In an exam, it is well worth considering whether a firm's marketing approach is ethical. Examiners do not assume that businesses always do the right thing.

Exam insight

Effective marketing is about getting the right marketing for the particular product for the particular business. Just as the business needs to understand its market to tailor its marketing you need to understand the business in the question to tailor your question.

Key Terms

Brand image – a name or symbol that customers easily recognise

Target market – the group of customers that a business wants to sell to

Test yourself

1 What is marketing? (2)
2 What are the advantages of effective marketing? (4)
3 Why do businesses need market knowledge? (3)
4 Why does marketing need to be integrated with the other business activities? (4)
5 What are the key features of efficient marketing? (4)
6 Is it ethical to aim advertising for crisps and fizzy drinks at young children? Explain your answer. (8)

Unit 36 Niche versus mass marketing

What?

Niche marketing

Niche marketing is tailoring a product to a small market. A niche market is a segment of a larger market. Many small firms start off by targeting small niches. As they are only able to sell to a small market, there are no cost savings from mass production. This means that niche products are generally sold at a higher price. Customers are willing to pay more for something they see as being different or exclusive. Niche products are likely to be less price sensitive, therefore price elasticity will tend to be low.

Mass marketing

Mass marketing is selling products that have wide appeal. This may be on a national basis, such as the soft drink Irn Bru (mainly Scottish, but with reasonable sales in the rest of the UK). Or the mass market may be on a global scale. If you travel to the Far East or to South America, in all but the remotest areas you will be able to buy a McDonald's burger and wash it down with a can of Coca-Cola. These two companies have achieved what most businesses can only dream of: they have produced products that have global appeal and recognition.

How?

- *Mass production* – mass marketing requires mass production. The product must be able to be produced in quantity and at a price that will appeal to a large number of consumers.
- *Efficient distribution* – if mass marketing is to succeed the product has to be available to a large and diverse group of customers. There needs to be a well-developed and efficient distribution system. The growth of supermarkets has brought many products to a mass market.
- *Effective promotion* – for mass marketing to work, the product must have universal appeal. It is no good producing millions of a product if customers don't want it. Most successful mass marketers have backed their products with extensive promotional campaigns. Some take full advantage of the global market by using the same advertising campaign in all of the countries in which they trade – with occasional modifications for language or cultural reasons.

Why?

When a business achieves a high level of sales it gains benefits. Its unit production costs should fall (*economies of scale*). This means that it can cut its prices. As sales increase, so will customer recognition. This makes it more likely that the brand will become established.

Brand recognition

Brand recognition is important for businesses as it gives the product many advantages. For example:
- it is easier to persuade retailers to stock the product;
- smaller discounts need to be given to retailers;
- customers are more likely to make repeat purchases and less likely to try out a competitor product.

Mass marketing can also **benefit the consumer**. When the Japanese electronics group Sony announced that it was entering the digital radio market the price of digital radio sets fell. This is because competition among manufacturers increased, leading to more competition between retailers. The customer hopefully gets the benefit of increased competition as well as lower prices resulting from lower costs.

When?

Firms may use niche markets as an introduction to a market or as a way of introducing new products in an existing market. Some firms will stay and be successful in their niche markets.

Decisions about mass marketing or niche marketing will depend on the particular firm and the marketing circumstances surrounding its products and its marketplace. Standard Chartered turned its back on the mass market in Cameroon. It limits its personal bank accounts to a minimum balance of £2,200 and business accounts to £5,500. For the vast majority of local people this is an impossible figure. This move away from mass marketing is based on profitability. The company has recognised that because of the particular circumstances in this market they are better off targeting a smaller but more profitable group of customers.

Firms are increasingly aware of the risks in treating customers as one large group. Customers are more sophisticated and have more spending power. Globally the mass marketers have also recognised that while brand recognition is desirable they need to be more sensitive in their marketing campaigns in non-western countries. These campaigns are now often focused on the country's culture rather than trying to sell a western lifestyle.

Exam insight

Mass marketing does not necessarily just mean high sales. It is about the product having wide appeal. Some firms achieve high sales by offering many niche products, such as BMW.

You should not assume that mass marketing is the aim of every firm. Many very successful businesses thrive on profitable niches – sometimes worldwide, such as Mercedes. Think carefully about the products and nature of each business.

Themes for evaluation

There is no 'one best way' to market your products. For some firms sticking to a profitable niche may be the best bet. In fashion-oriented sectors, mass marketing can be a mistake, as success may lead to over-exposure. The fashion conscious may then find a new product or label to support. Bill Gates did not become the world's richest man by niche marketing. His Microsoft company has a 90 per cent share of the world market for personal computer operating systems. Mass marketing blew away the niche market operators.

Application

A good example of niche market success is the Morgan car company. A family business, it produces fewer than 750 cars each year. The soft-top sports cars are considered by many to be old fashioned and even uncomfortable. Despite this, customers are prepared to wait, sometimes for up to three years, to own one. Demand always exceeds supply. It is difficult to know why this company has remained successful. It is probably because the product remains exclusive as so few cars are produced.

Application

The fashion industry is a perfect example of a market that has both mass marketing and niche markets. At the one end there are the fashion houses such as Chanel who make individually designed clothes for very wealthy women. At the other end are the high street names such as Primark and New Look that are cheap and cheerful and appeal to the mass market.

Key Terms

Economies of scale – cost savings due to an increase in the scale of production
Price elasticity of demand – a measure of how sensitive demand is to price changes
Price inelastic – the product is not very sensitive to changes in price; demand for a price-inelastic product will fall by a lower percentage than the price rise

Test yourself

1 What is meant by mass marketing? (2)
2 How may customers benefit from mass marketing? (4)
3 Which products are best suited to a niche market? (4)
4 How might a large firm use niche marketing? (4)
5 Outline two reasons why Morgan cars should keep away from the mass market. (6)

Unit 37 Designing an effective marketing mix

AQA Business Studies for AS Revision Guide

What?

The marketing mix is a marketing tool. It helps businesses to market a product successfully. The marketing mix focuses attention on the elements needed to carry out a marketing strategy successfully. A successful mix will produce customer satisfaction and help to achieve the marketing objectives.

It consists of four factors: product, price, promotion and place.

Product

A product is something that is offered to the market. Understanding the product, customers and competitors will help to ensure that the marketing strategy is the correct one to maximise sales.

Price

Price plays a critical part in marketing activity. Incorrect pricing policy could:
- lose customers – if the price is not 'right' customers will buy rival products;
- lose revenue – obviously lost customers mean lost revenue. Revenue can also be lost if the price is too low. An understanding of price elasticity of demand will help businesses to make correct pricing decisions.

Promotion

This is about communication. It is about telling potential consumers about a product. The aim is to persuade customers to buy the product.

Place

This is about availability. It includes the physical place, availability and timing.

How is it used?

The marketing mix is a tool that can be used by any business. Marketing managers look at each of the ingredients in the mix. They decide what marketing actions need to be taken under each of the headings. A new business can use this to help develop ideas about how and where to market the product or service. In reality a new business start-up may do little more than hand out leaflets or make a few telephone calls. As the business grows there may be need for more sophisticated marketing. The marketing activity will be constrained by the budget available.

For each market situation there will be an *optimum combination* of the ingredients based on a balance between *cost and effectiveness*.

The ingredients need to work with each other. A good product poorly priced may fail. If the product is not available following an advertising campaign the expenditure is wasted.

Where?

The focus of the marketing mix will vary according to the market that the firm is operating in. Industrial markets are different from consumer markets.

Where one business is supplying another (*industrial markets*) the key factors may be price, reliability, quality and availability. The product may have exact specifications agreed with the customer. Businesses purchase these products in order to produce their own products for the market. They will have concerns about cost, reliability, quality and availability. There will be less scope for modifying the product.

The *consumer market* supplies the final consumer. It is a much larger and more complex market. It is more likely to be affected by psychological as well as real factors. Hence the use of quirky advertising campaigns and pricing at psychological points such as £9.99.

In order to understand their market, businesses need to know who their customers are and to understand their buying habits.

Customers can be categorised by:
- spending power;
- age;
- gender.

The differences in customers and buying habits result in many 'markets within markets'. These are known as *market segments*. Each segment will require its own marketing mix. The fashion industry is an example. At one end, cheap, cheerful with mass availability. At the other end exclusivity and quality of workmanship are important.

How?

In order to understand their market businesses look at:

Buying habits

Most purchases fall into two categories:
- Convenience goods – these are bought frequently.

They include most non-durable goods. They are consumed when used. They can be:

- regular purchases
- impulse purchases
- emergency purchases.
- Shopping goods – the customer will take longer to choose. They include durable goods such as cars and household goods. They are used over and over again.

The type of consumer

Customers can be categorised in several ways. Such as by:

- *Spending power* – customer expectations and buying patterns vary with spending ability. Lower income households will look for less expensive hotels with family-sized rooms. Higher income families will look for more exclusive locations and better facilities.
- *Age* – there are some products such as toys or sheltered housing that are age specific. Businesses sometimes modify the product to make it appeal to other groups. Johnson and Johnson repositioned its baby skin products. It changed its promotion to encourage women to buy for themselves.
- *Gender* – many products are gender specific. If the product is sold as 'unisex' there will be a larger market. Calvin Klein sells perfumes for men and women.

But

The ingredients are not equally important

In most cases the product is the vital ingredient. No amount of marketing effort will make a poor product succeed. However a good product without good support may also fail.

Application

Woolworths, the High Street retailer with 800 shops employing 30,000 closed its doors for good in January 2009. It went into administration in November 2008 with debts of £385m.

It was started in 1879 in Liverpool by an American, Frank Winfield Woolworth. Everything was priced at sixpence (2.5p) and it was a huge success. So much so that eventually almost every town in the country had a store in the High Street.

Most analysts blame Woolworths' failure on a lack of focus. There was no clear product line – they tended to sell bits and pieces such as sweets, DVDs, stationery and toys. The interiors of the stores were dull and badly organised. The brand identity was dated. They were also unable to compete with the supermarkets on prices. So they were no longer seen by the public as a cheap place to shop.

It was not the credit crunch that finished off this High Street giant but a failure in its marketing mix. Wrong products in dull stores, bad availability and unable to compete on price – all contributing to a poor brand image.

Themes for evaluation

The marketing mix has been a part of the language of business since the 1950s. Many firms find it useful as a tool for looking at the whole marketing effort rather than just the promotional aspects. So which is the most important ingredient? Obviously a poor product rarely sells for long and it is often said that a good product sells itself. How important each factor is will depend on the business and its market. For this reason alone the marketing mix cannot be considered in isolation. For it to be useful it needs to be backed by good market analysis and clear marketing objectives and strategies.

Exam insight

Avoid repeating general textbook knowledge about the four Ps. Focus on the aspects that are relevant for the particular business in the case study. Try to make specific points such as: 'This particular small business needs to boost product sales by having a wider promotional campaign, as customers lack awareness of the product'.

Key Terms

Industrial markets – businesses that sell to other businesses
Marketing objectives – marketing targets and goals that the firm has for its products
Market segment – a smaller part of a larger market

Test yourself

1 What are the four ingredients of the marketing mix? (4)
2 What are the advantages of a good marketing mix? (4)
3 Which of the four Ps might be the most important for a new small producer of healthy soft drinks? Briefly explain your answer. (8)
4 How might Volvo market its lorries to an industrial customer such as Tesco? (4)
5 What is meant by a market segment? (2)

AQA Business Studies for AS Revision Guide

Unit 38 Product and product differentiation

What?

A product is something that is offered to the market. Businesses need to understand what the product is and what it means to the consumer.

A product can be:

- a good – such as a washing machine or shampoo;
- a service – such as accountancy or hairdressing;
- a place – such as a tourist destination;
- a person – such as a football player or pop star.

Products are not just physical things, they do something for the customer. Mobile phones are not just communication devices, they are also fashion accessories. Look at Nokia's range of interchangeable mobile phone covers.

Products provide both tangible and intangible benefits.

- *Tangible benefits* are those that can be measured. Cars have different performance levels. A Ford Focus will not give the same speed performance as a Porsche 911.
- *Intangible benefits* cannot be measured. They include things such as pleasure, satisfaction or peace of mind. Haagen Dazs' ice cream advertising does not emphasise the nutritional value of the ice cream. It concentrates on building an image for the brand. Building society advertisements emphasise security (an intangible benefit) above convenience (a tangible benefit).

Why?

Understanding the type of product is important. Businesses will need a different marketing strategy to sell a chocolate bar than a washing machine. For the chocolate bar the availability and the wrapping may be important features. For the washing machine, design and performance are more likely to be significant to the customer.

How?

Good marketing means developing products that 'fit' the market. They need to be designed correctly and then developed to keep pace with market changes. Businesses use market and product research to tailor products to customer requirements.

Market research

Market research is essential. It will help to understand the customer and the product. It will tell the business:

- who the customer is;
- how the customer makes their purchasing decisions;
- what the customer wants from the product;
- if there are gaps in the market;
- what rival products are in the market;
- what competitors are doing.

Product research

Product research concentrates on the product in order to:

- produce new products;
- modify existing products.

The role of new products

New products are important to businesses. They give competitive advantage. They bring new customers. New products may come from product research. They may have been developed to fill a gap in the market. When a new product is developed it should take account of market and customer requirements. Test marketing is a useful tool. The product may be launched in a small area to test customer reactions. Modifications can then be made before the final launch.

Managing existing products

Once a product is in the market the business needs to monitor customer and competitor reaction regularly.

It is essential that the product is developed using this feedback.

- This will maintain the life of the product.
- It will ensure that it does not get overtaken by rival products. Car manufacturers introduce new models on a regular basis. They also modify their existing models continually. These modifications keep the product 'fresh' in the eyes of the customer.

Product differentiation

In order to attract customer attention, businesses try to make their product different from those of rivals. The thing that makes the product different is known as a *unique selling point* (USP).

Be careful not to give a general answer about products and product differentiation. Focusing on the business and the product in the question will give you those valuable marks for application and analysis and enable you to make specific evaluative comments.

Why?

In a highly competitive market it is essential to make the product stand out from its rivals. It also:

- reduces buyers' price sensitivity – if the USP is something customers value they will not be so concerned about price comparisons;
- can create brand loyalty, which increases customer awareness. It makes the product easier to sell and can contribute to higher profits as higher prices can be charged.

How?

Some products are easier to differentiate than others. The secret is to find the modification that will have the most customer appeal. Understanding what customers want helps to ensure that the modifications are effective. When digital television was first introduced manufacturers kept adding more complex features to the boxes. This differentiated their products in a highly competitive situation. Some manufacturers realised that customers wanted a machine that was easy to use. This has now become a standard product feature.

Modifications can be made to:

- the design, such as shape or colour like in the Apple iPod;
- the performance, such as adding extra features or making the product easier to use;
- service levels, such as improving after-sales care or the guarantee period.

Businesses may also modify existing products to make them attractive to a different market segment. This may be just repackaging. Products sold to overseas markets will often require repackaging. In other cases the product may be altered. Heinz introduced a range of tinned products with lower sugar content to appeal to the health conscious customer. These are sold alongside its normal range.

Application

Clearasil is a skin care product aimed at young people between the ages of 11 and 24. It has used catch phrases such as 'visibly clearer skin in three days' and 'blitz the blackheads' to target its market and to successfully differentiate it from other skin care products.

Kate Moss designed a range of clothing for Topshop. When the shops opened the result was a scrum with the products flying out of the shops. Clearly Philip Green had found an excellent way of differentiating the brand.

Key Terms

Brand loyalty – when customers make repeat purchases of a particular product because they recognise/value the brand
Marketing strategy – the medium- to long-term plan to meet the marketing objectives
Price sensitivity – how customers react to price differences between similar products

Themes for evaluation

Critics argue that there are too many products in the market and that resources spent on promoting products would be better spent on improving products and service to customers. Businesses would argue that they do continually try to improve the product and that this is one of the best ways of ensuring sales and retaining customers.

There are also arguments about the ethics of persuading customers to pay a higher price for something that is essentially the same as a similar product. Do consumers get something more than the product when they become loyal to a brand?

Test yourself

1 What is a product? (2)
2 What is the difference between an intangible and a tangible benefit? (4)
3 What is the difference between market and product research? (4)
4 Why is it important to understand the product and its market? (4)
5 What is a unique selling point? (2)
6 List two reasons why it is important to differentiate a product. (4)
7 Think of a highly successful product that you know and outline the reasons for its success. (6)

Unit 39 Product life cycle and portfolio analysis

What?

The product life cycle describes the pattern of sales of a product over its lifetime. Normally sales increase slowly after a product is launched. This is known as the *introduction* period. If the product becomes more widely accepted sales will rise. This is the *growth* phase. Eventually sales will level off as the market becomes saturated and demand for the product is satisfied. The product is now said to be at *maturity*. At some point sales will begin to *decline*.

The diagram below shows the four main stages of the life cycle, plus the development stage. During this period the sales of the product are obviously zero. It is useful to include this stage when looking at the relationship between product life cycle and cash flow.

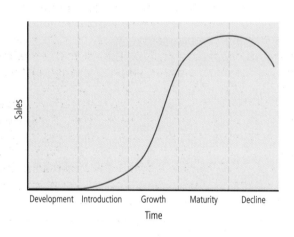

Fig. 39A: Product life cycle diagram

Why?

Each product or brand will have its own life cycle. Some are very long, such as manufactured cigarettes, which were 'born' in Britain in 1871 and enjoyed their sales peak in 1971. Sales today are about half the 1971 level. Other life cycles are short, such as toy or fashion crazes. The Pokemon craze lasted less than two years. Firms need to have a good idea of whether a new brand's life is likely to be long or short before deciding on a marketing strategy. Pricing decisions, for example, may be very different – with a skimming approach adopted for short life-cycle products, but penetration seeming wiser for those expected to have a long life.

How useful?

Businesses need to understand not only what is happening to their sales pattern but also why change is taking place. The product life cycle is a useful tool but only if managers really understand their products. If sales are falling this may be the start of the decline stage, but it may just be a short-term event that is happening in the market such as increased competitive activity. Knowing why change is occurring will help the firm to devise an appropriate strategy.

What next?

Marketing support is often used to alter the product life cycle. A well-focused marketing campaign can boost the initial level of sales following a product launch. It can also help to speed up the growth of sales. The maturity stage is usually the most profitable stage of the life cycle, so firms try to extend this period using extension strategies such as:

- selling the product to a new market segment;
- finding other uses for the product;
- changing the marketing mix.

Not all products go into decline. Maltesers enjoyed their best-ever sales year in 2008 – 70 years after product launch!

Cash flow and the product life cycle

When a business is developing a product, it will have expenses but no revenue. This can be seen on the diagram on the next page as a negative cash flow. As the product is introduced, revenue will start to increase but cash flow may still be negative, as the business needs to spend money to promote the product. As sales grow the need for this marketing support may diminish and so cash flow will become positive. If the product needs support to maintain its maturity stage then cash flow may again dip.

Product life cycle and capacity

Especially when launching a new product, firms need to ensure that they have the production capacity available if the product should enter a rapid growth stage. Failure to satisfy the market could damage the product image or as in the case of the iPhone it could

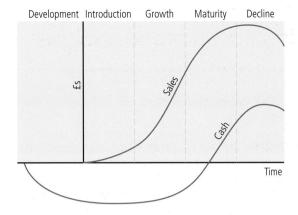

Fig. 39B: Product life cycle diagram and cash flow diagram

make the product more desirable. Firms need also to be aware that less capacity will be needed when the product reaches the decline stage and they may need to take steps to avoid idle capacity.

What is a product portfolio?

Most firms have more than one product. The range of products that they sell is known as their product portfolio. Firms need to be aware of each product within this portfolio. They need to understand what contribution each product is making to sales and profits. Firms clearly want the best mix of products. Portfolio analysis will help firms to choose which products are worth investing in and which may no longer deserve support.

How?

One tool that is useful in helping firms to analyse their portfolios is the Boston Matrix. This looks at a firm's brands in relation to two key factors:

1 What is the market (or sector) share?
2 What is the rate of growth within that market/ sector?

The results are then plotted on a diagram according to the market share and market growth for each brand.

Products are classified in four ways.

1 *Cash cow* – a cash cow product has a high market share with low to average growth in the market. These products provide a steady income to the business and their profit can be 'milked' to provide cash support for 'rising star' or 'problem child' products.

2 *Rising stars* – these products have a high market share in a growth market. Their future potential makes them obvious candidates for heavy marketing support.

3 *Problem child* – a product with a low market share in a growing market. Although the market may look inviting, these products have disappointed. The firm will need to decide if a new marketing strategy can save the product or if it will prove too expensive.

4 *Dogs* – these products have a low market share in a static or declining market. In most cases the costs of reviving these products outweigh the likely returns. They are therefore allowed to die when they fall below their break-even point.

Having identified how the products are performing in their market this information can be used to take appropriate action. Can the dogs be saved? What can be done about the problem child?

Application

At one time it seemed as though everyone was wearing Crocs, the roomy, colourful plastic shoes. In their first seven years the company sold 100 million pairs and in 2007 made a profit of $168 million. They were so successful that they were able to float on the US Stock Exchange and were able to raise more than $200 million. But everything has changed and in 2008 the company made a loss of $185 million. So what happened? Analysts suspect that the prime reason for the decline is simply a change in taste. Crocs have reached the end of their life cycle.

Dell, the US computer firm, has managed to increase its share of the computer market even though the market has been very sluggish. It has done this by using an aggressive pricing policy. It has also launched a new range of digital music players and televisions. Dell has recognised that its core products, computers, are operating in a mature and saturated market.

Themes for evaluation

Although there is agreement that it is useful for firms to gather knowledge about their product portfolio and the life cycle of individual products, it is important that managers understand what the information is telling them. They need to be able to make sensible and cost-effective decisions based on the information. In reality the information gathered will probably be more useful in understanding why something has happened rather than as a planning aid.

Test yourself

1 What are the five stages of a product's life cycle? (5)
2 What may explain why some products such as Coca-Cola never seem to go into decline? (4)
3 How can firms extend the life of their products? (3)
4 What is meant by a product portfolio? (2)
5 What is the Boston Matrix and how might it help a firm? (6)

Unit 40 Promotion

What?

Promotion is a general term that covers all of the marketing activity that focuses on letting the customer know about a product and persuading them to buy that product. **It is not just about advertising**. Promotion should be:

- informative;
- persuasive;
- reassuring.

Which?

One way of looking at promotional activities is to divide them into two categories: those that stimulate short-term sales and those that build long-term sales.

Building long-term sales

- *Branding* – one of the best forms of promotion is branding. Branding is the process of creating a distinctive and lasting identity in the minds of consumers. Establishing a brand can take considerable time and marketing effort but once a product brand is established it becomes its own means of promotion. A successful brand has many advantages:
  - it enables the business to reduce the amount spent on promotion;
  - customers are more likely to purchase the product again (repeat purchases);
  - it is easier to persuade retailers to put the products in their stores;
  - other products can be promoted using the same brand name.
- *Persuasive advertising* – this is where the company uses advertising to create an image. It is often accompanied by a slogan that hopefully will be remembered and associated with the company and its range of products, e.g. L'Oréal 'Because you are worth it'
- *Public relations* – this is about getting the company name or product known without spending on media advertising. It includes activities such as sponsorship of sport or arts and contact with the media to get favourable reviews of products.

Boosting short-term sales

- *Sales promotions* – these range from on pack offers and competitions to in store offers such as 'buy one get one free' (BOGOF). Whilst effective at boosting

sales customers may stock up so the effect may be temporary.
- *Direct selling* – potential customers are approached directly. At one time this would be done by door-to-door salesmen. Nowadays the main mechanism for direct selling is telesales. It is an expensive method and is only worthwhile if the product has a high value such as double glazing.
- *Merchandising* – this involves setting up special displays, demonstrations, free samples or special offers in shops. The business will pay the store to have an area dedicated to their product but additional sales can make up for this.

How?

Businesses will not just use one method of promotion. They will have a mixture of activities, such as TV advertising, newspaper advertising, direct mail shots, in store promotions. These are known as the **promotional mix**. The mix of promotional activities will depend on the:

- *size of the market* – if the market is large the business will primarily use advertising through the mass media. If the market is very small this method will obviously be too expensive and inefficient. Direct marketing or selling will probably be best.
- *type of product* – a consumer product will require different promotion to an industrial product.
- *cost/available budget* – a small or new business is unlikely to be able to spend large amounts of money. This means that some forms of promotion such as TV advertising are out of range for the business. They need to find cheaper alternatives such as local advertising and direct marketing or selling.

Getting the promotional mix right will require the business to understand the nature of its product, its customers and its competitors. Good **market research** will provide the essential information to make the right decisions about the promotional mix.

The more information the business has about its customers and its competitors the easier it will be to develop an effective promotional campaign.

- If the business knows who is likely to buy the product it can determine its target audience and specifically target that group.
- If the business understands why customers are choosing a rival product it can specifically design promotional material that addresses these issues.
- If the business understands what makes its product

attractive to customers it can use this knowledge to reinforce the promotional message.

Market knowledge is always important if promotional activity is to be effective. However it is **vital for a new business**. If the business is unable to target the right market segment or to persuade customers to buy the product then the promotional expenditure will be wasted. Ultimately no sales means no business.

But

Promotion needs to be effective

Being effective means getting a balance between cost and results. The business needs to monitor promotional activity to see if it is having the desired effect. A prime time TV advert may reach a huge audience but is ineffective if it does not increase sales.

Why?

Promotion is **vital for a new business**. How else will customers know that they exist and what their products are? Existing business may need to do less promotion.

The importance of promotion will depend on:
- the competitiveness of the market;
- availability;
- how easily the product can be differentiated in the market;
- the stage of the product life.

In **industrial markets** where one business is selling to another there may be less need for promotion. This is particularly true where a business is supplying products to the customer's specification and has established an ongoing relationship with the buyer.

Exam insight

Promotion is about telling the customer about the product and persuading the customer to make a purchase. It is therefore vital when answering a question on promotion to consider the business, its product and the market. Answers should consider the different promotional methods available but should concentrate on those that are suitable for the particular business.

Key Terms

Consumer product – a product sold to the public
Industrial product – a product sold to another business
Mass market – a large market
Market research – gathering information about customers and competitors
Market segment – a smaller part of a larger market

Application

In March 2007, Lloyds TSB became the first official British sponsor of the London Olympic Games in 2012. It is thought to have cost Lloyds TSB £80m. It will be the only high street bank to have marketing rights for the London 2012 Olympics and will be able to use the Games' logo in its promotions. The bank will help sell and distribute tickets to the Games when they go on sale in 2011.

London 2012 chief executive, Paul Deighton, said, 'London 2012 is a once in a lifetime opportunity for businesses in the UK to access the powerful benefits associated with staging the Olympic and Paralympic Games. The commercial value of a London 2012 partnership will be realised long before the opening ceremony in 2012, and can be sustained as a legacy for decades after the final race is won.'

Themes for evaluation

Promotion is generally considered to be a good thing for businesses to do. But is it? How do they know if it is money well spent? It is very hard to measure the effect of promotion.

There are also questions asked about the ethics of promotion. Is it right to have sweets for sale by the till or to advertise toys during children's programmes?

Test yourself

1 What is promotion? (2)
2 Why is promotion essential for a new business? (4)
3 Why is it important to do market research before deciding on promotional activity? (4)
4 What is meant by the promotional mix? (2)
5 Why should businesses monitor the effect of their promotional activity? (4)

Unit 41 Pricing

The price is the amount paid by the customer for a good or service. Pricing is a vital element in marketing strategy. It must fit in with the business objectives and the overall marketing mix.

Why?

Pricing is important because it is one of the main links between the customer (demand) and the producer (supply). As part of the marketing mix it plays a strong role in marketing the product. For most customers price is a fundamental part of the buying decision. The importance of price will depend on:

- *Customer sensitivity to price* – consumers have an idea of the correct price for a product. They balance price with other considerations such as:
  - the features of the product such as its design and performance;
  - the real or perceived quality of the product;
  - customers' income.
- *The level of competitive activity* – customers have more choice in a competitive market. Businesses may use price to differentiate their product. They may also use price as part of their promotional activity. For some products such as branded goods the price is kept higher to reinforce the brand's value. In a monopoly the business is able to charge higher prices.
- *The availability of the product* – if the product is readily available, consumers are more price conscious. Scarcity removes some of the barriers to price. This can be seen in the art world where huge prices are paid for paintings. Shortage of the product forces the price up.

Pricing is important because it determines business revenue

Unlike the other ingredients in the marketing mix it directly contributes to revenue:

Sales revenue = price per unit × number sold

Price has a direct influence on demand

If the price is not right the business could:

- *Lose customers* – if the price is too high sales may fall and revenue will be lost. Understanding price elasticity of demand (see Unit 42) will help a firm to understand how price increases affect demand and revenue.
- *Lose revenue* – if the price is too low customers may feel that it is an inferior product. If the price

is lower than the market will take, the firm will be missing out on revenue.

Pricing involves a balance between being competitive and being profitable.

When?

Businesses need to make pricing decisions when they launch a new product. There are two main strategies for new products:

- *Skimming* is used when the product is innovative and there is no competition. The price can be set at a high level, thus allowing the firm to recoup the development costs.
- *Penetration pricing* is used when launching a product into an existing market. The price is set lower than that of competitors to gain market share.

Which?

Firms also need to manage prices throughout the product life. The lowest price a firm can charge is set by costs. These will be manufacturing or purchasing costs and costs such as distribution, administration and marketing. The market determines the highest price that can be charged. There are several different pricing methods:

- *Cost-plus* – this is a commonly used method among small firms. A mark-up is added to the average cost. This method ensures that some profit is made, as long as sales meet expectations. This is because all costs are accounted for in the price.
- *Contribution* – as long as the selling price is above the variable costs, the business receives a contribution to covering its fixed costs. Therefore the business may charge high prices to those that can afford to pay more and lower prices to people who can afford less (or want the product less). This is the basis for price discrimination, as used in rail and air travel. A second-class return Virgin Rail ticket from London to Manchester can cost between £20 and £180, depending on who is travelling and the time of day. Virgin Rail try to sell as many tickets as possible at £180, but know that students paying £20 are still making a contribution to fixed costs and profit. Price discrimination means charging different people different prices for the same product.
- *Competitive* – this method sets the price in relation to competitors' prices, i.e. it is a 'price taker'.

Prices may be lower or the same as competitors, depending on the marketing strategy.

- ○ Set at the market level: used in highly competitive markets such as retail petrol. If Shell charges 2p per litre more than Esso, sales will suffer badly. Businesses want to avoid a price war that will lower returns, so all price at the market level.
- ○ Set in relation to the price leader: for example, if Heinz Beans are priced at 52p per tin, HP will price at 48p. If the Heinz price rises, so will HP. The company knows it cannot price alongside Heinz, because HP sales would fall sharply.
- *Predatory* – this is pricing below cost, with the deliberate intention of driving weaker competitors out of the market. This is not legal, but it is very difficult to prove intent. Consumers love low prices, so few people or politicians complain if a price war is raging.

Pricing tactics

Pricing should be closely linked to the marketing strategy. Once this has been determined there are many different pricing tactics that can be used, such as:

- *Loss leaders* – prices are set deliberately low. This is to encourage customers to buy complementary goods that generate profit.
- *Psychological pricing* – prices are set at a level that seems lower. A price of £19.99 seems lower than £20.
- *Promotional pricing* – a range of tactics which includes special offer pricing – 'buy one get one free' or offers made for a period of time or to clear stocks.

Exam insight

Take care not to confuse price and cost. Price is what the customer pays and therefore what the business charges the customer for the goods or service. Costs are what the business pays for its raw materials, etc.

When answering a question on pricing, take care that the suggested pricing methods are realistic for the business and its market circumstances. A long list of possible pricing methods will not gain high marks.

Themes for evaluation

There is no one correct pricing method. Most businesses use a combination of pricing strategies. Although the theory gives the impression that firms choose their pricing methods, in reality many firms base their pricing on cost plus or what the market will take. What is vital is that in the long term, revenue must be greater than costs. One of the interesting things about pricing is that customers often have an intuitive feel for the correct price. Market research is a useful tool to connect to this customer 'feel'.

Application

Ryanair, the low cost airline, has perhaps gone too far with its suggestion of charging customers to use the 'loo' during flights. It has always priced its tickets competitively. Now it has adopted a policy known as unbundling. It has separated out the various services that it provides and charges separately for each of these. So passengers have to pay to check in baggage and for in flight food and drinks. Now it is suggesting that using the toilet facilities could also be unbundled. Many people think this is a step too far and it may well make passengers look more carefully at the total cost of their flights with Ryanair rather than just at the low flight price.

Businesses use pricing strategies in many different ways. Madonna's album *American Life* went straight to the top of the charts in its launch week in April 2003. The instant success was helped by aggressive price reductions. It was sold by some of the larger chains for half the normal retail price. Yet in 2008 on her 'Sticky and Sweet' world tour, ticket prices of up to $500 created gross takings of a record $280 million.

Other businesses price high as a demonstration of the confident, upmarket image they wish to portray, such as Mercedes, BMW, Chanel and Diesel jeans.

Key Terms

Average price – total cost divided by the number of units
Complementary goods – products bought in conjunction with each other such as shavers and razors
Economies of scale – cost savings made possible by increased production or sales
Elasticity of demand – a measure of how sensitive demand is to changes in other factors such as price or income
Monopoly – a market dominated by one supplier

Test yourself

1 How does the availability of a product affect pricing? (3)
2 What is the relationship between price and revenue? (3)
3 Name and explain two pricing strategies for new products. (4)
4 Why might a firm offer a discount? (3)
5 What is meant by cost-plus pricing? (2)
6 What problems might occur if the price is too low? (5)

Unit 42 Price elasticity of demand

Elasticity of demand shows the effect on demand of a change in the price of the product. Using elasticity of demand enables a business to see what will happen to demand for their products when the price changes.

What?

Price elasticity of demand tells the firm how demand for the product can be expected to change with changes in price. It gives the business an indication of how *sensitive* demand is to changes in price.

The formula used to calculate price elasticity of demand is:

$$\text{price elasticity} = \frac{\%\ \text{change in quantity demanded}}{\%\ \text{change in price}}$$

If the percentage change in demand is greater than the change in price, i.e. the price elasticity is greater than 1 (>1), then the product is said to be *price elastic*.

If the percentage change in demand is less than the change in price, i.e. the price elasticity is less than 1 (<1), then the product is said to be *price inelastic*.

Why are some products price elastic and others price inelastic?

Price elastic products tend:
- to be widely available;
- to be undifferentiated from other products;
- to have many acceptable alternatives (have substitutes);
- not to be classed as necessities.

They will include products such as sun and sand holidays, and retail petrol brands.

Price inelastic products tend:
- to be in short supply;
- to be necessities;
- to be branded;
- to be innovative.

They include basic products such as electricity but also designer/fashion clothes or distinctive cars such as the Mercedes Smart car.

Why?

In order to plan and successfully market their products businesses need to know what factors affect demand and how sensitive demand is to those factors. As price is a very sensitive element in determining demand it is vital to know how customers will react to price changes.

The business may want to raise prices. However, it needs to understand what effect this will have on sales and profitability. If the product is price elastic then revenue will fall if prices are raised.

Exam insight

Percentage change is calculated as:

$$\frac{\text{Change}}{\text{original figure}} \times 100$$

If sales were 100 units and increased to 120 then the percentage change would be:

$$\frac{20}{100} \times 100 = 20\%$$

If the price of the product was increased by 15% and the demand for the product fell by 30% then the price elasticity would be:

$$\frac{-30\%}{+15\%} = -2.$$

Every firm wants to predict the likely effect on sales of a change in the price of its products. If you know the elasticity and the percentage change in price you can calculate the percentage change in demand. You just alter the elasticity formula so that:

$$\%\ \text{change in demand} = \%\ \text{change in price} \times \text{price elasticity}$$

Example

A firm is selling 1,000 items at £10 each. Currently revenue is £10,000 (£10 × 1000). If the price is increased by 20% to £12 and the price elasticity of demand is 2 then the demand for the product will fall by 40% to 600, i.e. percentage change in demand = 20% × 2 = 40%.

Now revenue will be £7,200 (£12 × 600), i.e. it falls by £2,800.

Clearly for this firm a price rise means a loss of revenue so this strategy makes little sense. Management needs to consider other ways of raising income and in this case a price cut would actually increase revenue.

If the firm has some idea of how demand reacts to price changes then it will be able to forecast sales better and so enable production to meet demand. If a firm stimulates demand by reducing prices it needs to ensure that it has sufficient product to meet that demand; if it does not it will lose revenue.

How to change?

The ideal situation for a business is to have products that are price inelastic. They can make the products more inelastic by:
- differentiating them from other products in the market (ideally by adding a USP, a unique selling point) – this may be done by product development or a change in presentation such as packaging;
- encouraging brand loyalty (for example, better quality or a good after-sales service);
- removing competition (for example, taking over a rival firm).

But

Price elasticity can only be worked out using historical data. It can therefore only be a guide to what might happen in the future. It is impossible to know for certain that the change in price was the only factor affecting sales. Other factors such as competitor's actions may also have affected the results.

Application

For a number of years many of the world's largest airlines operated a high price policy. They were able to rely on brand image, shortage of competition and business customers who were insensitive to price. In recent years that has all changed. More competition – especially from low priced, no-frills airlines – has meant that there are alternatives and, with more leisure travel, customers are more price sensitive. Business users have also woken up to the cost-cutting possibilities of the low cost airlines. As a result, many major airlines are now offering cut-price seats. What the airlines have experienced is a change in the price elasticity of demand. An apparently price inelastic product has become elastic.

Exam insight

Note that all price elasticities are negative numbers. This is because a price rise pushes demand down and a price cut pushes demand up. In the exam, the price elasticity figure will always be given with a minus sign.

Key Terms

Price elasticity – the extent to which demand changes when the price is changed.
Price elastic – a product that is highly price sensitive, i.e. price elasticity is greater than 1.
Price inelastic – a product that has low price sensitivity because customers see it as distinctive.

Themes for evaluation

How valuable is price elasticity?

Calculating and using elasticity can help in making business decisions, but must be treated with some caution. Like many business tools it is a guide and helps a business to gain an understanding of what is happening in the marketplace. For example, if a product is very price elastic then the firm may be able to work on ways in which to reduce the elasticity so that it has more flexibility and control over pricing policies.

Do businesses really use elasticity?

Elasticity is often thought to be a theoretical rather than a practical business tool. However, it is vital that businesses are at least aware of what the market reaction will be to changing prices. Without this basic understanding the business could make costly marketing decisions.

Test yourself

1 Explain the meaning of the term 'price elastic'. (3)
2 State the formula for calculating price elasticity of demand. (2)
3 A firm increases its price from £20 to £22 and the demand for its product falls from 120,000 to 102,000. Calculate the price elasticity of demand and state whether it is elastic or inelastic. (5)
4 Why would a firm not want to raise prices if its product was price elastic? (2)
5 For each of the following identify one example:
   (a) a price inelastic product
   (b) a price elastic product. (2)
6 State two things that a firm can do to make its products more price inelastic. (2)
7 A firm sells 100,000 units of a product that is estimated to have a price elasticity of –2. If the firm decreases the price of its product from £5.00 to £4.50 what will be the new sales volume? (6)

Unit 43 Place

What?

This is about availability. It includes the physical place, availability and timing.

The right place is where the customer is. Manufacturers need to get their products displayed in the right retail outlets. There is great competition for 'shelf space'.

Products also need to be available when the customer wants them. Getting the product to the customer at the right time is an important part of the marketing effort.

The key questions facing firms are:

- What are the best outlets for reaching potential customers?
- How can I convince those outlets to stock my products?
- What is the most effective way to get my products to those outlets?

Where?

The decision on where to place products is often very difficult for new businesses. They may have very little experience of the marketplace. If they are launching an innovative product such as a robotic lawnmower, would they want it in every garden centre, DIY outlet, department store and Argos catalogue? That would depend on their overall strategy and of course how many products they can manufacture. If they are the only supplier, which is often the case with innovative products, they should set a high price to enjoy high profit margins to recoup the initial investment (skimming the market). In which case it would be better to limit the products to department stores or to sell directly on the internet. Later, they could bring the price down and strike a deal with a mass retailer like Homebase.

Persuading retailers to stock a product is never easy. For the retailer, the key issues are opportunity cost and risk. As shelf space is limited, stocking a particular chocolate bar probably means scrapping another. Which one? What revenue will be lost? Will one or two customers be upset? ('What! No Coffee Walnut Whips any more!')

The other consideration is risk. A brand new chocolate bar endorsed by a supermodel may be a slimmer's delight, but high initial sales may then flop, leaving the shopkeeper with boxes of slow-moving stock.

How?

Another important issue to consider is the distribution channel. In other words, how the product passes from producer to the consumer. Sold directly, as with pick-your-own strawberries? Or via a wholesaler, then a retailer, as with newspapers bought from your local shop?

There are three **main channels of distribution**.

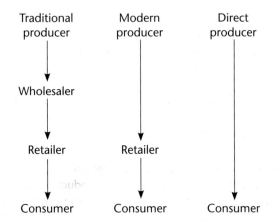

Traditional

In the days before hypermarkets and superstores, shops bought their stock from wholesalers, who in turn bought from producers. The profit mark-up applied by the 'middle man' added to the final retail price, but wholesalers had many other advantages. They 'broke bulk', meaning that they might buy a container load of Andrex, but be happy to sell in boxes of 48 packs to shopkeepers. This ensured that small shops did not need to hold high stock levels.

Modern

Sainsbury's, B&Q and WH Smith do not buy from a wholesaler. They buy direct from producers and then organise their own distribution to their outlets. Their huge selling power gives them huge buying power. Therefore they are able to negotiate the highest discounts from the producers.

Direct

Years ago, door-to-door selling was an important distribution method. Today, direct selling is more likely to be through websites. Some companies such as Dell only sell their computers direct to the consumer. By cutting out the wholesaler and the retailer, Dell is able to offer low prices for up-to-date machines. Initially this gave Dell a big advantage over High Street firms such as Dixons and PC World who have huge overheads to pay. Internet selling has become very popular. Most of the high street stores now offer their products direct to the customer using the internet. Even supermarkets now encourage shoppers to shop online and to get their goods delivered directly.

For *manufacturers* selling this way means that they 'cut out the middleman' so keeping more of the profit for themselves.

But

Place is about availability so it is also important that stocks are available when customers want them. If a product is not available buyers may switch to an alternative brand. Getting the *distribution* right is therefore an important part of getting the place right.

Exam insight

Getting the product to the customer will vary from business to business and product to product. Not all products sell in supermarkets. Take care to consider the elements of place that are right for the particular business and product. Remember as well that place is also about having the goods available so consider if there are distribution issues.

Key Terms

Overheads – the costs involved in keeping the business running. Also known as fixed costs

Retailer – a business that sells directly to the final customer

Wholesaler – a firm that buys from the manufacturer and sells to the retailer

Themes for evaluation

Deciding where to sell your product is a big decision for all businesses and there is no one solution. Retailers will clearly want to have a high street presence but what about other businesses? The growth of industrial units alongside motorways show that for some businesses it doesn't matter where they are placed as long as they have good communication links so they can get goods to the customers. One of the big issues of the day is the growth of web-based sales. Should they fight it or join it?

Application

Amazon is a typical web-based business. Originally selling books over the internet they now sell a vast variety of goods, some through linked sites to other sellers. As they have no direct customer contact they do not need a retail outlet such as in the high street. They do need a good distribution network and their site next to junction 13 on the M1 is ideal.

Hotel Chocolat started life as a web-based retailer but as the business expanded they decided to sell their products on the high street and their shops can now be seen in most town shopping centres.

Test yourself

1 What does the term 'place' mean? (2)
2 Why is it more difficult for a new product to get shelf space? (4)
3 What would be a suitable place to sell
   (a) family holidays
   (b) funky jewellery? (4)
4 Why have internet sales grown so rapidly? (6)

Place

Unit 44 Marketing and competitiveness

What?

Competitiveness is about how a company performs compared to its rivals. Some markets are highly competitive – supermarkets battle against each other for customers. Washing powder manufacturers are continually trying to convince customers that their product is better than that of their rivals. Other markets may be less competitive. Marketing is a significant element in competing with other firms.

Which?

All markets are different and the level of competition differs.

In an *extremely competitive market* there will be many products competing against each other. These products will be very similar so as far as the customer is concerned there is little difference between them.

A less competitive situation is an oligopolistic market. In an *oligopoly* several larger firms divide the market between them.

Another situation is a *monopoly* where one firm effectively dominates the market.

Of course there are many possible variations within these catagories. Train operators may seem to have a monopoly, but they are competing against other forms of transport, such as road and air travel.

The greater the level of competition the more the business needs to do to make it stand out from its rivals.

How?

In order to compete in a market a firm must attract customers and keep them. It needs to make its product or service stand out from those of its rivals. It needs to convince customers to ignore competing products.

Marketing plays an important role in this. The following will be helpful in a competitive situation:

- *Design* – a good product that is well designed will attract customers.
- *Packaging* – attractive packaging can get the buyers' attention.
- *Quality* – poor quality products lose customers.

- *Unique selling point* – having a USP will distinguish the product from its rivals.
- *Brand image* – this keeps customers loyal and attracts customers even when there is no real difference in the product.
- *Lower prices* – when products are very similar customers will often use price to make their choice.
- *Promotion* – all forms of promotion contribute to bringing the product to the buyers' attention and hopefully persuading them to buy the product rather than that of a rival.

But

Marketing is important as a competitive tool but remember that it is not the whole picture. An inefficient firm that has high costs will not be able to offer competitive prices and be profitable. Poor customer service may drive away more customers than any special offers gain.

Being competitive involves the whole of the business. Other company issues that contribute to competitiveness are:

- *Management* – good management means that the whole business is run in a cost effective manner. This will allow more flexibility on pricing, more funds available to improve the business and to spend on marketing activity and will contribute to a positive public image of the firm.
- *Investment* – modernising machinery will help to cut costs and enable better quality.
- *Training* – having efficient and knowledgeable staff contributes to lower costs and better customer service which both give a competitive advantage.
- *Operational efficiency* – good investment, good staff and good management all contribute to operational efficiency that keeps down costs and enables the production of good quality products.

However

One of the important considerations in competitiveness is the actions of other competitors. By its very nature a competitive market means that the business is not operating in isolation. There may also be other external factors that affect the firm's ability to compete. Increasing globalisation factors such as lower wage costs may make it harder to compete with imported goods.

Application

During the recession in 2008/9, shoppers inevitably turned to the discount supermarkets such as Aldi and Lidl. These shops offer a more limited range of goods but at lower prices. The growth at these stores greatly outstripped that of the traditional stores such as Tesco and Asda.

The big supermarkets had to fight back and they have managed to remain competitive and bring back many of those customers. Asda ran a round pound approach – selling many items for £1. Tesco introduced a new 'discounter' range priced between its value range and its own-label products. Waitrose, the upmarket supermarket, also joined in with its Essentials range.

Key Terms

Globalisation – the trend for increased international trade

Monopoly – a market with only one supplier

Oligopoly – a market with several large companies who dominate sales

USP – unique selling point. A feature that makes a product different to similar products

Exam insight

Every business and product faces a unique market. Tailor your answer to the business or product discussed in the question. What is the nature of the business and its market? Suggest solutions that are specific in this case. Remember competitiveness is not just about marketing. For a firm to be competitive it needs the whole business to be working well.

Themes for evaluation

In global markets there are cost advantages that can be gained from moving production abroad. Think of call centres and toys made in China. Is it ethical for firms to move production overseas in order to reduce costs?

In crowded markets is it right that firms use marketing to persuade customers to buy their product rather than that of a rival?

Test yourself

1 What is meant by a competitive market? (2)
2 What is an oligopoly? (2)
3 Explain the term 'product differentiation'. (2)
4 What is market share? (2)
5 List and explain two marketing activities that might contribute to competitiveness. (6)
6 Explain why operational efficiency is important for competitiveness. (6)

8 Exam success

Unit 45 A grade business concepts for AS level

The exam is about your ability to **use** business theory. It is not enough to know the theory. An A grade student will be able to apply the theory to answer questions in a way that is applied to the subject of the question and to show some judgement.

There are several business concepts that you need to understand and be able to apply to different situations.

Opportunity cost

This is the cost of what is being given up in order to do something. As resources are limited there are always choices being made. Moving a call centre overseas may significantly reduce costs but it may do this at the expense of customer satisfaction.

Objectives

This is what the business wants to achieve. It is generally considered that all businesses have the objective of making profit. Is this true?

Strategy

This is the plan for achieving the business objectives. How the business is going to get there. An important distinction is between plans and tactics. Tactics are the short-term actions to deal with day-to-day situations.

Risk

This is a fundamental concept for all enterprises. An understanding of the risk involved and how this can be minimised is a useful way of looking at business issues. Market research and good sound financial analysis are good tools for analysing and reducing risk.

Distinguishing between cash flow and profit

This is vital for any finance issues. Unit 19 gives a full explanation.

Competitiveness

In almost all markets businesses will face rivals. If they are to succeed they need to be able to cope with this. Remember that this is not just about price. There are other **non-price factors** such as quality, availability, design and customer service that can be equally important.

In context

You cannot get an **A** grade if your answer does not relate to the business or issues in the question. It will help you to do this if you:
● read and understand the material and spend time analysing any numerical or graphical information;
● read the questions twice, with care.

Understand the issues

If you do not understand the business story you could waste precious marks by failing to apply your answer to the context, or answering the wrong question. Make sure you understand the issues. You need to ask yourself:
● What sort of business is it?
● Large or small?
● Plc or private company?
● Manufacturer, retailer or in the service industry?
● What are its objectives?
● Do a quick SWOT analysis. Think about the firm's strengths, weaknesses, opportunities and threats.
In this way you will get a picture of the business and its issues, which will help you to focus your answer on the business (application).

Understand the question

Many students lose marks in exams because they do not answer the question that is being asked. Make sure that you understand the questions.
Identify the key words:
● Key 'subject' words such as price, competitors, and stakeholders are important. This is what the question is about.

- Key 'doing' words such as describe, analyse, discuss, and evaluate will tell you what you need to do. Anything involving discussion or evaluation or a decision about a situation always means that there are marks for evaluation in the mark scheme.
- Don't forget the little words, such as the difference between 'a business' (you can write about any one) and 'the business', i.e. the one in question. Or the difference between being asked 'how' or 'why' the business is facing problems. Look out for clues that relate the question to a point in time or to something that the business has done (before/after).

Look at the marks allocated:

- Generally it is fair to assume that 2-mark answers will require a direct response based on knowledge. This is a content or knowledge mark.
- For a 4-mark answer you will often be expected to show your knowledge of the subject but also to put your answer in the context of the case study. This is application, e.g. you may be asked about sources of finance for the business in the case study. So you might say: 'For a small business such as this the options are limited to…, etc.'
- For more than 4 marks you are likely to be expected to include analysis and evaluation.

Plan your answers

In most exams you will be awarded more marks for the depth of your answer. AQA papers are marked using a system that awards marks for content, application, analysis and evaluation.

What is content?

Content is about knowledge. Do not be afraid to state the obvious. It often helps to start your answer with a definition.

What is application?

Application is about applying the knowledge/subject matter to the situation. If asked about sales promotion think about what would work for this business in its particular competitive situation. If all you do is to talk about the theory you will only be awarded content marks. Another way to demonstrate application is by comparing the situation in the case study to a real life situation.

What is analysis?

Analysis marks will only be awarded if the answer is based on relevant theory used in the context of the question. General answers, say about motivation issues, will get some but not many marks. You need to show which motivation theory is relevant to this business or its present situation and why.

Analysis explores the issues. It asks 'why?' It says 'however' or 'but'. Or you might use 'if' or 'in some cases'. For example:

- 'Cash flow forecasts are a useful business tool – however as they are estimates they are only as good as the figures they are based on.'
- 'Just-in-time methods of stock control are good because… however they may also cause difficulties for the business such as…'

What is evaluation?

Evaluation is about judgement. If you are asked to compare two possibilities for the business then evaluation is easier. You should analyse the two options and then make a judgement about why one is better than the other for this business.

Your judgement should be based on the arguments that you have put forward and should always relate to the business in question.

Finally do not forget the QOL

On every A-level paper that has a written component, marks are awarded for quality of language (QOL). These few marks should not be ignored! That one extra QOL mark might just tip you into the higher grade. The other reason to give QOL some thought is that well-written work is more likely to make and analyse points with clarity. A-level marking is positive marking, which means that the examiner is looking for good points. If your work is clear and easy to follow it will be so much easier to award those marks. QOL scores can be improved by:

- Using sentences and paragraphs. Try to keep sentences short. Avoid using a lot of 'ands' and 'buts' in a sentence. Use a paragraph to explain one idea.
- Sort out the spelling. If you don't know the difference between 'there' and 'their', that's poor. In Business Studies, though, we care even more about whether you can spell 'lose', 'strategy', 'opportunity' and 'morale'.

Unit 46 Tackling the BUSS1 exam

You should read this unit with a past BUSS1 exam paper beside you, available on the AQA website.

Format of the paper

The BUSS1 exam lasts for 75 minutes. It carries 60 marks. You should spend around 1 minute for each mark a question is worth – therefore, spend 5 minutes on a 5-mark question and 12 minutes on a 12-mark question.

The paper is based on one business scenario. The questions are split in two – Section A consists of fairly short questions and calculations and carries 20 marks. Section B carries just three questions for which you must write much longer answers. Section B carries 40 marks.

What you should do

Understanding this scenario and using it in your answers is vital to achieving good marks. You should therefore read the scenario very carefully before starting to answer the paper. The scenario will include some numerate data, so take a little time thinking through what the numbers are actually showing you about the business and its performance.

Section A

Top grade students must aim to score at least 16 out of 20 on this section and probably expect to score 20/20. There are four basic types of question in Section A.

Definitions

Starting with the phrase 'what is meant by', these two or three mark questions simply want you to give a concise and accurate definition of a piece of terminology from the specification. Revision is the key here – know all your key terms and you will know the answers. Often an example will help to clarify your definition – do not be afraid to give a relevant example to illustrate your definition.

List, state or identify questions

These are designed to test your ability to remember various listed options that your teacher will have covered in class, such as motives for becoming

an entrepreneur or different methods of primary research. There is no need to write a lot for these one or two mark questions – write the bare minimum to make yourself understood. The main pitfall is not ensuring you read the question carefully, since they will often start by referring to something done in the scenario and ask you to state a possible alternative. Too many students state only the thing mentioned in the question – so a question asking you to state a type of government support for entrepreneurs other than the grant received by the firm in the question will award no marks for writing grants.

Calculations

There will be a couple of calculation questions in this section. Always start a calculation question by stating the formula you have learned that will be used to answer the question. This will immediately earn you knowledge marks for the question before you write down any numbers. Look carefully in the business scenario for the right data – check that you pick the information for the right year. Then do your sums. Make sure you show your workings step by step. This is not because that's what teachers always tell us to do in maths – it's so that if you make a small error, the examiner has proof that you followed the right method, even with a small mistake and can therefore award you most of the marks available for that question. Wrong answers often drop just one of four or five marks if the workings are clear.

Read the question carefully and do exactly what it asks you to do, so if it asks for the change in the break-even point from one year to the next, work out both break-even points and also work out the change – failure to do so will cost you marks.

The final advice on calculations is to stick strictly to the 'mark a minute rule'. Do not get sucked into spending ages trying to get a calculation right. After two or three minutes you have probably already scored the most marks you are going to get. Sticking doggedly to a calculation until you have cracked it will do huge damage to the time you have left to answer the higher mark questions later in the paper.

Knowledge and application question

Generally the final question in Section A carries between 4 and 6 marks and expects you to demonstrate how your knowledge can be applied to the scenario. Start the question by defining accurately the business terminology in the question. Then make just two different points, but be sure to write enough to make it clear what you mean (explain your point) and ensure that you explain why that point is relevant in this particular business – it is this that will gain your application marks. It may help you get application marks if you quote a couple of words or a phrase from the scenario to illustrate your answer. Never quote more than a phrase at a time – sentence after sentence copied from the case will earn no marks and waste your time.

Section B

Section B contains just three questions. However, these questions will be the ones that really determine how good a grade you end up with. Top students will answer each question well, scoring marks for each exam skill being tested in each question. Before starting these, it is probably worth quickly skim reading the scenario again to refresh your memory of the context in which you must answer the questions.

Knowledge, application and analysis question

The first question in Section B will test your knowledge, application and analytical skills. Stick to your basic exam technique and start your answer with a definition of the business term in the question. Again, make only two different points – business studies exams are never about making lots of different points, they are far more interested in what you can do with a small number of points. For each point you make, choose one that will be especially relevant for this business. Explain what you mean fully and look to pick specific aspects of the scenario when explaining why you feel this point is especially relevant to the business in the scenario.

To earn the analysis marks, you must build a chain of logic from each point you make. Generally this will involve moving on to consider the consequences of the point you have made, and perhaps the knock-on effects of those consequences. For other questions, you may be asked to look into causes, as well as effects of something that happened in the scenario. You will find the word 'therefore' and the phrases 'as a result' and 'this means that' especially helpful when trying to build a chain of logic.

Do not waste time writing a conclusion since there are no marks available on this question for evaluation.

Knowledge, application, analysis and evaluation questions

The final two questions in section B test all four of your exam skills. Once again, start your answer by looking for a definable piece of terminology within the question, and define it. Then stop for a few moments to think about how you will be able to build two contrasting arguments given the way the question is phrased. Questions beginning 'do you think' expect you to consider both sides in writing before you offer your judgements. Questions asking you to discuss will again expect a two-sided discussion. Other stimulus words for these questions are 'to what extent' and 'evaluate'.

For some questions you will be expected to argue for and against a certain proposal within the question. On other occasions you may be expected to 'discuss several factors' or 'decide on which factor was most important'. In both cases you need to build a logical two-sided argument. You must not build an eight-sided argument by trying to make too many different points. Especially on questions that ask you for 'the most important factor', there is often a temptation to resort to listing as many factors as you can think of. This is a foolish approach. You should never need to consider more than three different points in these questions, usually two will be enough to earn top marks. What matters is how well you apply each point to the context and build up a logical chain of argument. With two, or three (but not four) points made, you should then start to write your conclusion.

A conclusion on a business studies question should never be a mere summary of what has gone before. The job of your conclusion is to show the examiner that you can make a clear judgement based on the arguments you have put forward earlier in your answer. You should therefore refer only to the arguments you have put forward – a conclusion is not the place to make brand new content points. The trick is usually to show that you can weigh up the relative importance of the two arguments you have put forward and decide which is the more convincing.

If time permits, it is often sensible to reread your answer before you start to write your conclusion since it will give you a moment to consider which of your arguments is strongest. It can also help to avoid a common phenomenon – concluding that the last point you wrote about is the most important, simply because it's the only one in your head when you come to start your conclusion. Good conclusions will always restate the question being answered. This technique helps to ensure that your conclusion answers the question you are supposed to be addressing. Often, after ten minutes of application and analysis, your mind remembers a subtly different question to the one on the paper, and you wind up writing a conclusion to the question in your head, not the one on the exam paper.

Finally be sure to make a clear judgement such as:
- I agree/disagree with the statement in the question.
- Yes she should/no she shouldn't open a second branch.
- The MOST important factor is…

This final type of judgement is the one which students most often get wrong. A question that asks you to 'discuss the main benefits of setting budgets for the business' expects a judgement in which you choose the most important benefit, having analysed two or three key benefits for that firm. It does NOT expect you to discuss any drawbacks – reread the question, it's quite clear. However, in the desire to find a way to make a judgement, weaker students may choose to ignore the question on the paper and answer one which has evolved in their head by saying that the benefits outweigh the drawbacks.

Final advice

Your performance in Section A will not gain you a top grade but it might lose one. Set your standards high for section A – you can afford to drop 3 or 4 marks but no more if you plan to get an A grade. Top students prove themselves in Section B and they do it, partly, by editing their answers before they begin to write. Section B answers featuring the phrase 'and also' are likely to turn into little more than a list of underdeveloped points that fail to trigger marks for application, analysis and evaluation. Your business exams will never reward you for lots of different points. Instead, top marks are achieved by students who take their time over a very few points on each question and know what they are expected to do with each point they make.

Unit 47 Tackling the BUSS2 exam

You should read this unit with a past BUSS2 exam paper beside you, available on the AQA website.

Format of the paper

The exam carries a total of 80 marks and lasts for 90 minutes. You should write for 1 minute for every mark allocated. That leaves you with 10 minutes of reading, thinking and planning time.

The exam is split in two questions. Each of the two questions carries 40 marks. Each question is based on a different business scenario. You should have 5 minutes to read each scenario and start to think carefully about the particular issues for that business.

Each question is usually split into four parts. The first part of each question will only test knowledge and application. At least one of the two will be a calculation. The second part of each question carries slightly more marks (usually 7 or 8) and tests knowledge, application and analysis.

The final two parts of each question will be worth 11 or more marks and will test all four of your exam skills – knowledge, application, analysis and evaluation.

Question 1	Question 2
a) Tests knowledge and application, possibly via a calculation	a) Tests knowledge and application, possibly via a calculation
b) Tests knowledge, application and analysis	b) Tests knowledge, application and analysis
c) Tests knowledge, application, analysis and evaluation	c) Tests knowledge, application, analysis and evaluation
d) Tests knowledge, application, analysis and evaluation	d) Tests knowledge, application, analysis and evaluation

Calculation questions

Always start by stating the formula you have learned that will be used to answer the calculation question. This will immediately earn you knowledge marks for the question before you write down any numbers. Look carefully in the business scenario for the right data – check that you pick the information for the right year. Then do your sums. Make sure you show your workings step by step. This is not because

that's what teachers always tell us to do in maths – it's so that if you make a small error, the examiner has proof that you followed the right method, even with a small mistake and can therefore award you most of the marks available for that question. Wrong answers often drop just one of four or five marks if the workings are clear.

Read the question carefully and do exactly what it asks you to do, so if it asks for the change in the profit margin from one year to the next, work out both profit margins and also work out the change – failure to do so will cost you marks.

The final advice on calculations is to stick strictly to the 'mark a minute rule'. Do not get sucked into spending ages trying to get a calculation right. After three minutes you have probably already scored the most marks you are going to get. Sticking doggedly to a calculation until you have cracked it will do huge damage to the time you have left to answer the higher mark questions later in the paper.

Knowledge and application written questions

Part a) questions do not need you to demonstrate analysis or evaluation. Therefore do not waste your time trying to do them. There is no need to develop long chains of logic or write a conclusion – the examiner cannot give marks for these on a question that does not offer analysis or evaluation. Instead, stick to the tried and tested methods for earning knowledge and application marks. Start the question by defining accurately the business terminology in the question. Then make just two different points, but be sure to write enough to make it clear what you mean (explain your point) and ensure that you explain why that point is relevant in this particular business – it is this that will gain your application marks.

Knowledge, application and analysis questions

Stick to your basic exam technique and start your answer with a definition of the business term in the question. Again, make only two different points – business studies exams are never about making lots of different points, they are far more interested in what you can do with a small number of points. For each point you make, choose one that will be especially relevant for this business. Explain what you mean fully, and look to pick specific aspects of the scenario when explaining why you feel this point is especially relevant to the business in the scenario.

To earn the analysis marks, you must build a chain of logic from each point you make. Generally this will involve moving on to consider the consequences of the point you have made, and perhaps the knock-on effects of those consequences. For other questions, you may be asked to look into causes, as well as effects of something that happened in the scenario. You will find the word 'therefore' and the phrases 'as a result' and 'this means that' especially helpful when trying to build a chain of logic.

Do not waste time writing a conclusion since there are no marks available on these questions for evaluation.

Knowledge, application, analysis and evaluation questions

Once again, start your answer by looking for a definable piece of terminology within the question, and define it. Then stop for a few moments to think about how you will be able to build two contrasting arguments given the way the question is phrased. Questions beginning 'do you think' expect you to think both sides in writing before you offer your judgements. Questions asking you to discuss will again expect a two-sided discussion. Other stimulus words for these questions are 'to what extent' and 'evaluate'.

For some questions you will be expected to argue for and against a certain proposal within the question. On other occasions you may be expected to 'discuss several factors' or 'decide on which factor was most important'. In both cases you need to build a logical two-sided argument. You must not build an eight-sided argument by trying to make too many different points. Especially on questions that ask you for 'the most important factor', there is often a temptation to resort to listing as many factors as you can think of. This is a foolish approach. You should never need to consider more than three different points in these questions, usually two will be enough to earn top marks. What matters is how well you apply each point to the context and build up a logical chain of argument. With two, or three (but not four) points made, you should then start to write your conclusion.

A conclusion on a business studies question should never be a mere summary of what has gone before. The job of your conclusion is to show the examiner that you can make a clear judgement based on the arguments you have put forward earlier in your answer. You should therefore refer only to the arguments you have put forward – a conclusion is not the place to make brand new content points. The trick is usually to show that you can weigh up the relative importance of the two arguments you have put forward and decide which is the more convincing.

If time permits, it is often sensible to reread your answer before you start to write your conclusion since it will give you a moment to consider which of your arguments is strongest. It can also help to avoid a common phenomenon – concluding that the last point you wrote about is the most important, simply because it's the only one in your head when you come to start your conclusion. Good conclusions will always restate the question being answered. This technique helps to ensure that your conclusion answers the question you are supposed to be addressing. Often, after ten minutes of application and analysis, your mind remembers a subtly different question to the one on the paper, and you wind up writing a conclusion to the question in your head, not the one on the exam paper.

Finally be sure to make a clear judgement such as:
- I agree/disagree with the statement in the question.
- Yes she should/no she shouldn't open a second branch.
- The MOST important factor is…

This final type of judgement is the one which students most often get wrong. A question that asks you to 'discuss the main benefits of setting budgets for the business' expects a judgement in which you choose the most important benefit having analysed two or three key benefits for that firm. It does NOT expect you to discuss any drawbacks – reread the question, it's quite clear. However, in the desire to find a way to make a judgement, weaker students may choose to ignore the question on the paper and answer one which has evolved in their head by saying that the benefits outweigh the drawbacks.

Final advice

Read each scenario carefully. Your application and evaluation marks will be impossible to achieve without answering the question about the business in your exam paper. You should hopefully find that you have lots of possible answers in your head for each question. Take a moment to pick the two points that are most relevant in this situation and only write about those. Good performers in these exams are brave – they will never be the first person in the room to start writing, and will usually choose deliberately to not write about some points that they have learned in the classroom because they are irrelevant to the firm in the exam paper's scenario. And finally…

Don't leave any of the questions out. Write down something for every question – the first three marks on any question are always easier to gain than the second three marks.

Answers

Unit 1

Test yourself

1 Willing to take a risk; determined; have persuasive abilities; good at building relationships.
2 *Primary* – agriculture, fishing, mining. *Secondary* – manufacturing, processing raw materials. *Tertiary* – service industries such as media, banking, tourism.
3 What is given up in order to do something. For example, investing in a new business means giving up a holiday or a new car.
4 Gives a return for time, effort and money invested. External finance will not be possible without some return on the investment. Provides funding for business growth.
5 Understanding the risk involved.
6 Good planning and research. Research will confirm if the idea can succeed and planning will ensure that everything has been considered before starting out.

Unit 2

Test yourself

1 A section of the market where there is no supply of the goods or services that are needed.
2 A small specialised section of a larger market.
3 Small budget research. Looking around, observation, talking to people, trying goods out on family and friends.
4 Can gain business experience. Less likelihood of failure as idea already proven. Less entry costs. Easier to borrow.
5 Business Link is a government service to help new businesses.
6 New businesses are good for the economy: more tax if business is successful; less benefit payments. If business succeeds it may employ more people and make even more contribution to the economy.

Unit 3

Test yourself

1 So that they get paid when people use the material. To stop others copying their work without permission.
2 Material can be easily copied and transmitted. It is very difficult to police the internet.
3 It gives it a distinguishing feature that makes it stand out in the marketplace. This will encourage customers to choose the product. Sales will be higher and higher prices can often be charged.
4 A patent means that the idea is protected for 20 years. This means that the inventor has a monopoly on the idea. This means that a high price can be charged for the product especially if there are no alternatives.
5 Think about the pros and cons of the matter. Research is very important and very expensive so that drug companies need to generate enough income to pay for this. Drugs are necessary for health and may save lives so there is an argument that they should be available at the lowest possible price. Perhaps governments should pay the research costs.
6 It may stop others copying your idea so means less competition. With a patented idea you know that you have some time before others can copy the idea so can spend more time and money setting up the business.

Unit 4

Test yourself

1 Personal information, objectives, marketing plan, production plan, financial plan.
2 The banks, etc. will be able to see how the business will work. They will be able to evaluate the risk of lending to the business. If there is a business plan they will know that the entrepreneur has thought through the business idea.
3 The planning process will help the owner to think through their ideas for the business very carefully. It will help to identify any problems and to clarify what needs to be done to get the business up and running.
4 Allows an objective assessment of success; could identify the major areas where the business failed or exceeded expectations during the year.

Unit 5

Test yourself

1 Whether they will need limited liability. Whether they want to be the only owners or would they benefit from raising more money by selling shares to other shareholders. If they expect the business to grow in the near future they may well then need to take advantage of the limited liability offered by Ltd status.

2 Different initials in the name of the firm (Ltd is private plc is public). Only the plc can offer shares for sale to the public through the stock market. Ltds are likely to have shareholders who are more understanding of long term policies than plc shareholders, who are likely to be demanding a return on their investment immediately.

3 If owners have limited liability they cannot lose personal assets as a result of their business being sued for malpractice or wrongdoing. Suing a partnership means suing the owners themselves.

4 There is no need to follow any legal formalities, thus reducing legal fees and possibly allowing the start up to happen faster. As a café is unlikely to run up significant debts, the need for limited liability is less than would be found in, say a manufacturing start up.

5 Family firms may wish to retain full control over the business. Some firms do not welcome the short-termist pressure that often comes from a stock market listing. Some firms may not be willing or able to find the money required to float on the stock market. If there is no need for extra capital, there is little to be gained from a flotation.

Unit 6

Test yourself

1 A new business does not have any information about the market. It needs to know what demand is for its product or service, how much it can charge, etc. Market research will enable it to build a good business plan and to avoid costly mistakes.

2 *Primary research* is where the business gathers information for itself; *secondary research* is where it uses information that has been gathered by others.

3 *Quantitative research* is statistical information. It shows how many or how much. *Qualitative research* tries to find out why or how. It looks at the reasons why customers act in a certain way.

4 *Random sampling* – expensive to carry out properly; only useful if you want a cross-section of the whole population. *Quota sampling* – requires the consumer profile to be known in advance; still subject to bias,

e.g. interviewers selecting people who look friendly or unhurried.

5 Large enough to ensure that the sample is representative of the group being surveyed. Not so large that it is too expensive.

6 A good questionnaire will have:
   – questions that are focused on what the company is trying to find out;
   – questions that do not lead towards a particular answer;
   – questions that are clear and unambiguous;
   – questions that have closed answers, i.e. a choice of responses such as yes or no;
   – basic demographic information to enable a better analysis of the results.

Unit 7

Test yourself

1 By volume (quantity of a particular good) and by value (value of sales of those goods).

2 Saga Holidays – holidays for the over 50s, the leisure market.
Top Shop – High Street fashion, young, trendy, lower price, mass market.
British Gas – gas supply to industrial and consumer markets, the energy business.

3 Price
Income/level of economic activity
Actions of competitors
Marketing
Seasonal factors
Social changes
Changes in fashion

4 Sales of mountain bikes/all bicycle sales x 100 = 21,000/£40,000 x 100 = 2.5 per cent.

5 Which market, so that it knows who the customers are and how to target them.
The size of the market and the level of demand and the trends in demand. This allows the business to know if there is space in the market.
The nature of the market. What are competitors doing? All of this market information will enable the new business to make informed decisions when entering into a market.

Unit 8

Test yourself

1 Spending by the business on fixed assets.
2 Retained profit; sale of assets; from working capital.

3 Overdrafts – short-term flexible lending; short- and long-term loans.
4 Not paying immediately for goods and services from other businesses. Limited amount. If bills are not paid promptly businesses may be unwilling to trade with the firm.
5 Because it has no history; if it is in difficulty; if it is not profitable; if it already has high debts.
6 Loans; sale of shares; venture capital.

Unit 9

Test yourself

1 Cheaper than easy to reach locations, may not need customers to visit, for example Amazon.com.
2 Burger bars tend to rely on passing trade, a burger is more of an impulse purchase than a model-making shop, which relies on planned visits. Model-makers will set out on a specific journey to the model-making shop.
3 The firm may rely heavily on people to run its business – perhaps it is a service business, the firm may need staff with certain specialist skills.
4 a) Proximity to a supplier of apples since they will be bulky to transport; space may also be important to store the apple harvest; b) A broadband internet connection will be vital, so infrastructure is important, while skilled staff will be important, but may be able to work electronically from far away, customers may want to be able to visit so closeness to financial markets could be important; c) A cheap store will want cheap rent, whilst customers must be able to get to the store fairly easily.

Unit 10

Test yourself

1 Minimum wage; issuing contracts; registering with HMRC.
2 Part-time staff are contracted to work for less than 30 hours per week, but may have a permanent contract, whereas temporary staff have a fixed-term contract, stating when their employment finishes.
3 a) Temporary as the business is highly seasonal; b) Permanent because staff will need to be fully committed to the business to ensure they give excellent customer service, and may need to be trained; c) Temporary staff – since demand for these products will be short-lived, the firm will want to be able to reduce the size of its workforce easily once the Olympics are over.
4 Benefits include: greater flexibility if more children bring in packed lunches or eat off-site; the contractor

will have greater expertise at managing school catering than school managers. Drawbacks could include: lower levels of service with staff not fully committed to the school; possibly higher costs since the contractor needs to make a profit, while the school may be happy to break-even if run in-house.

Unit 11

Test yourself

1 Variable – car shampoo, sponges. Fixed – staff wages (if paid hourly), maintenance of equipment.
2 Total variable costs = £5 x 1000 = £5,000, so with £2,000 of profit, the other £5,000 of revenue must be fixed costs.
3 Total revenue was £10,000, of which half was profit so total costs must have been £5,000, leaving total variable costs of £2,000. If 1000 units were sold the variable cost per unit was £2.
4 a) Finding a cheaper supplier, possibly accepting a lower quality of materials, would help to reduce variable costs and therefore increase profit. b) The lower quality of materials will have an effect on the image of the firm's products. Attempts to change the quality of materials are unlikely to go unnoticed by customers who may stop buying from the firm. Alternatively, if the firm comes clean and cuts their selling price this would have an adverse effect on profit.

Unit 12

Test yourself

1 a) £6,000/(£5 – £2) = 2,000 units. b) 2,500 – 2,000 = 500 units.
2 Requires careful forward planning; helps to assess likely cost levels; can indicate the need for a change in strategy, pricing or purchasing. Sales are likely to be quite constant, so the analysis will be useful for quite a period of time.
3 Sales may be hard to predict in such a fast moving market; variable costs may alter significantly as technology advances; competition may hit sales.
4 Sales revenue – the number of customers turning up and paying to use their facilities. This will be complicated by differing charges for different activities. Variable costs will be minimal, but fixed costs such as staffing and maintenance will probably be easier to calculate than revenue.

Unit 13

Test yourself

1 The flow of cash in and out of the business.
2 A management tool that shows the flow of cash in and out of the business and summarises the expected cash balances of the business.
3 If the business does not have sufficient cash to pay its bills it may be faced with bankruptcy or insolvency.
4 In the short term having sufficient cash flow is vital. However, the business needs to be profitable in the long term.
5 To be sure that the business has enough cash to enable it to survive; will be able to repay the loan; can afford to make the interest payments.
6 Chasing debtors to pay on time will bring cash into the firm quicker and more predictably, while taking as long as possible to pay suppliers will keep cash in the business for longer. Reducing stock levels keeps more of the firm's working capital in the form of cash.
7

	January	February	March	April
Cash in	100	110	120	120
Cash out	90	110	130	100
Net cash flow	10	0	(10)	20
Opening balance	10	20	20	10
Closing balance	20	20	10	30

Unit 14

Test yourself

1 Focusing management time and attention on areas with significant budget variances.
2 Helps to control costs that will, by definition, be increasing if the firm is rapidly growing. Can allow delegation of spending power to ensure top bosses are not overburdened at a time of expansion.
3 Innovation may be hampered with people unwilling to take risks that could lead to budget overspends. Clever budget holders who can negotiate higher budgets may not need to keep their costs as low as necessary.
4 The ease of budgeting decreases as forecasting gets trickier. Firms manufacturing novelty items are likely to be selling different products for a short time at different times throughout each year and these short bursts of sales will be tough to predict accurately. This also makes it very hard to forecast costs accurately. A washing machine manufacturer may well find a far steadier pattern of sales during the year along with a more stable product portfolio.
5 Expertise; experience; instinct; market research.

Unit 15

Test yourself

1 Answers could include:
financial – get rich, make a comfortable living, make a specific level of profit; *personal* – be own boss, show what I can do, get out of boring job, be able to build something, avoid regretting a missed opportunity, build something for my family; *social* – any realistic objective which would make society better, perhaps environmental aims or helping the underprivileged.
2 *Within the entrepreneur's control* – poor stock control, poor staff recruitment or training, poor customer service, poor financial management. *Outside the entrepreneur's control* – arrival of new competitor, price cuts by existing competitors, suppliers failing to deliver.
3 a) Delays to supplies – may mean production cannot take place, meaning that customers cannot be served, meaning customers that you have fought hard to attract now go elsewhere, and are far harder to get back.
b) Unexpected increases in costs – may push costs higher than revenues, leading to a loss making business, BUT the thing that will hurt most in practice is the effect on cash flow, as cash flows may be higher than forecast, leading to a shortage of cash, and an inability to pay bills, leading to bankruptcy.
c) Unexpected changes in demand – lower demand than forecast would lead to lower sales than expected, perhaps with the need to slash prices to try to attract customers, but these low prices or the lower than expected demand, are both likely to lead to a shortage of cash, again, suggesting an inability to pay bills and possible bankruptcy.

Unit 16

Test yourself

1

	April			May			June		
	Budget £000s	Actual £000s	Variance £000s	Budget £000s	Actual £000s	Variance £000s	Budget £000s	Actual £000s	Variance £000s
Income	500	500	0	520	530	**10F**	520	510	10A
Expenditure	400	410	10A	410	410	0	410	**420**	10A
Profit	100	90	**10A**	110	120	**10F**	**110**	90	20A

2 Focusing management time and attention on areas with significant budget variances.

3 Revenues may be lower than expected, perhaps as a result of fewer customers than expected or perhaps they are spending less than forecast. Alternatively, costs may be higher than expected, perhaps the result of naïve forecasting by the owner or perhaps due to suppliers increasing their costs.

4 Rapidly growing firms may well see adverse cost variances, as they fail to allow for the increases in costs that stem from increased demand. Focusing on reducing adverse cost variances may actually stifle the firm's ability to maintain its growth rate as they attempt to limit spending. In such a rapidly changing market as software development, unexpected spending may be necessary to keep up with competitors in developing new, more advanced software. Focusing on avoiding adverse variances may force the firm to fall behind its rivals.

Unit 17

Test yourself

1 The flow of money into and out of the business.

2 Working capital is the cash held in the business. It is used to pay for day-to-day expenditure such as wages, raw materials and utility bills.

3 Not having enough cash can create problems with suppliers and lenders. It may cause the firm to miss opportunities and the firm may be unable to grow.

4 A firm can improve its cash inflows by:
   – getting goods to the market in the shortest possible time
   – getting paid as soon as possible
   – controlling debtors
   – factoring

5 A firm can solve a short-term cash flow shortage by:
   – using an overdraft
   – taking out a short-term loan
   – sale and leaseback of assets (possibly more suitable for a longer-term problem)

6 There is no 'right' level, it depends on the business – its liquidity cycle and its attitude to holding cash. If too little this may cause problems. If too much opportunities to invest and grow may be missed.

Unit 18

Test yourself

1 Branch X: Net profit margin £25,000/£125,000 x 100 = 20 per cent; return on capital = £25,000/£250,000 x 100 = 10 per cent

Branch Y: Net profit margin = £16,000/£200,000 x 100 = 8 per cent; return on capital = £16,000/£320,000 x 100 = 5 per cent.

Branch X is clearly most successful with a higher net profit margin and a higher return on capital.

2 Keeping fewer copies of each DVD in stock would reduce the cost of buying DVDs, however, this may lead to many unhappy customers who can't get newly released DVDs. Cutting back on staffing levels would reduce the cost of wages, but may lead to longer queues in-store and delays in putting returned DVDs back out on to the shelves, both of which are likely to reduce customer satisfaction. Cutting back on marketing costs would leave the business with less to spend promoting new deals to customers. This could be a real problem in a market being increasingly challenged by online DVD rental sites and more recent releases being available on paid for TV channels.

3 Cutting price should lead to an increase in the quantity

of products sold. If the price cut was small and the change in demand outweighed its effects, the extra units sold would make up for the reduced profit per unit. However, profitability measures the rate of profit made (roughly equivalent to profit per unit). Here is a numerical example to illustrate:

	Before price cut	After price cut
Units sold	100	140
Selling price	£10	£9
Revenue	£1000	£1260
Variable cost per unit	£5	£5
Fixed costs	£100	£100
Total costs	£600	£800
Profit	£400	£460
Net profit margin	40%	37%

Unit 19

Test yourself

1 Revenue is the total money raised from sales of a product. It is part of cash flow when the money is received by the business. Cash inflows are all cash that comes into the business. As well as revenue this may be loans or shareholder funds or cash from the sale of assets.

2 Seasonality may mean that there are times of the year when little cash is coming into the business but costs still have to be paid.

3 A healthy cash flow is vital to ensure that bills and loan repayments can be paid on time. This avoids the problems with suppliers and banks. Profit is vital in the long term as investors will want to get a return on the money they invested. The business may be able to live for a while without profit but in the long term it needs to be profitable.

4 The cash flow problems a profitable business might have are:
   – insufficient cash at start-up where outgoings are hard to predict
   – a change in sales may result in lower cash in
   – higher costs may result in cash out
   – a sudden unexpected event may require cash output

Unit 20

Test yourself

1 Controlling costs should enable a firm to generate a profit, while cash flow management will be easier if continual and accurate monitoring is taking place. Problems can be identified and prevented early, before they become threatening to the survival of the business.

2 Financial forecasts will be based on a number of assumptions relating to the future period to which they are related. Both internal and particularly external factors may be impossible to forecast accurately – for example, cost increases from suppliers or unexpected dips in sales caused by the arrival of a new competitor.

3 Arrange an overdraft to cover the period during which sales are low. Delay payment to suppliers, preferably with their agreement.

4 Expansion implies that costs will be increasing now, in the hope of increasing revenues at some point in the future. This generally means that cash outflows will increase some time before the firm is able to operate at the expanded level of output which would be the time that cash inflows would be expected to catch up with outflows. Of course, during this time lag, bills will still need to be paid and so for the period of expansion, cash will be critical, with profit taking a back seat until the expansion is complete.

5

	January	February	March
Cash in	100	110	120
Cash out	90	110	130
Net cash flow	**20**	0	**(10)**
Opening balance	10	**30**	**30**
Closing balance	30	30	20

6 Helps to plan for the future; may be needed to secure finance; identifies future cash flow problems early enough to take corrective action.

7 Factoring means selling a debt to another company who will provide roughly 80 per cent of the value of the debt in cash immediately and a further 15 per cent or so on collection of the debt.

8 Chasing debtors to pay on time will bring cash into the firm quicker and more predictably, while taking as long as possible to pay suppliers will keep cash in the business for longer. Reducing stock levels keeps more of the firm's working capital in the form of cash.

9 Trading profit; working capital; asset sales.
10 Share capital.
11 (Net profit/capital invested) x 100
12 Profit is an absolute number – a value measured in pounds (or euros or dollars). Profitability is the rate at which a firm makes profit on its sales. In other words it is the percentage of revenue that is left as net profit once costs have been deducted.
13 Assumes all output is sold; assumes revenue and variable cost lines are straight; it is only as good as the data used to construct it.

Celebration Cakes

1 The money available for the day-to-day running of the business – it will be in the form of stocks, money owed by customers and cash, but money owed to suppliers must be deducted before arriving at a final figure for working capital. Trading profit may make a contribution if their other business is generating sufficient profit. Any unused assets could be sold off, or even currently used assets could be sold and leased back. Money can be squeezed out of working capital, perhaps by reducing credit terms offered to smaller customers.
2 40,000 cakes per month.
3 Variable costs per unit may fall at higher levels of output as suppliers may be willing to offer bulk buying discounts (an economy of scale). This is especially true given the significant increases in purchasing levels implied by the story of the rapid rise of the Celebration Cake maker.
4 Possible solutions could include factoring the debts owed by the supermarkets (margins are high enough to cope with the factor's fee), increasing pressure on suppliers to offer more generous credit terms to L&H Davison or reducing stock levels in order to free up more cash (this firm's stock may well be at great risk of 'going off' if kept too long). Evaluative themes, such as suggesting that a combination of methods is likely to be more effective than trying to find one solution would be expected within your answer.

Nurwoo Noodles

1 Total revenue is the value of sales made, i.e. the quantity sold multiplied by the price charged.
2 Budgeted profit = £4,200. Actual loss = £300, variance is adverse = £4,500.
3 Budgeted profit margin = £4,200/36,000 x 100 = 11.7%; actual profit margin = (£300)/£30,700 x 100 = -1%
4 Closing the Bromley restaurant may be a hasty decision – external factors may have caused the weaker performance. Meanwhile, closing the restaurant will mean that it contributes nothing towards covering the company's total overheads, reducing the overall profit of the business.
5 Tighter budgetary control could have kept variable costs, such as ingredients lower – with lower sales fewer ingredients should be needed. Overheads and wages should have been kept lower with closer monitoring of costs. However, many of the problems stem from disappointing revenues and these are likely to be the result of external factors, such as a very hot summer, opening of competitors or health scares. Budgetary control tends to help on the cost side but revenues tend to be more influenced by factors outside management's control.

Unit 21

Test yourself

1 40 units per worker per month.
2 Better machinery; more motivated staff; better trained staff; better organised production process.
3 More customers can be dealt with in any given time by an operator, meaning that fewer checkouts need to be open. If the same number of checkouts are open, queues will be shorter meaning happier customers.
4 Some firms may feel that the route to increasing productivity lies in making workers work harder – reducing breaks, imposing output targets, etc. – all of which are likely to be unpopular. Other firms may decide that the only way to increase productivity is to increase the level of automation, replacing people with machines – again rarely popular with those staff being replaced. Finally, any firm that does manage to increase productivity will need to find a use for the extra output being generated, otherwise the increased productivity may simply be the key to laying off a certain proportion of staff.

Unit 22

Test yourself

1 a) A manager is responsible for a relatively high number of subordinates – probably more than 6.
 b) The route from bottom to top of the organisation's structure is long, with a relatively high number of layers/intermediaries to pass through.
 c) An organisation where decision-making power is kept at the top of the structure and not delegated throughout the organisation.
2 Flatter structures encourage delegation – just what tends to be needed in a creative workplace such as an advertising agency. A flat structure should also ensure that even senior managers have fairly regular contact with clients and are therefore able to keep a close eye

on trends within the market.

3 Confusion over whose instructions to follow may be the result of having two bosses. The more complex nature of such a structure could breed communication difficulties.

4 All staff know who their boss is and therefore who to go to in the event of needing advice. Clear chains of command ensure that coordination can be achieved.

Unit 23

Test yourself

1 Labour productivity is falling, labour turnover is rising. Falling productivity can be caused by aging machinery breaking down, by staff lacking motivation or by poorly organised production. Increasing labour turnover may be caused by dissatisfied staff leaving as a result of monotonous jobs or poor management. Increasing labour turnover may lead to increased recruitment and training costs, while the time taken to replace and train staff who have left may well lead to the reduction in productivity shown for the same firm. The reduction in productivity is going to increase the cost per unit, reducing the competitiveness of the company.

2 Labour turnover is a key indicator of management practices that are not working well. If the bulk of staff that are leaving are going due to natural wastage, such as retirement, the firm may not need to overhaul their management practices. If the bulk of leavers are going because they do not like working for the firm, action would be necessary.

3 Problems of measurement revolve around the number of different influences on employee performance, such as machinery and equipment being used, the amount of training being offered and the way in which they are managed and motivated. Of course, there are times when a firm with excellent people management may still lose their staff if they leave to gain promotions elsewhere. All in all the problem is that measurements of workforce effectiveness may well be skewed by factors outside the control of the firm's HR department.

Unit 24

Test yourself

1 a) Hiring new staff from outside the existing workforce to introduce fresh ideas and attitudes. b) Methods of choosing which applicants from a recruitment process will be employed.

2 To save money, because an interview can tell little about

how well a labourer will work.

3 Whether the firm has a simulator that can be used in off the job training; whether store managers are too busy to offer on the job training; whether the till has changed significantly from that the employee was used to using.

4 New roles may mean increased pay and status within the firm. Staff may also feel a sense of motivation as a result of the sense of achievement gained from learning new skills and as a result of feeling sufficiently valued by their employer to be trained in these new skills.

Unit 25

Test yourself

1 Paying people commission; time and motion study as echoed in benchmarking; scientific management – the use of quantitative decision-making techniques in business, such as price elasticity.

2 Accept that your workers are human beings and as such need to have their social needs met – set up a staff social club. Pay attention to your staff, take an active interest in how they are getting on.

3 *Physiological* – decent pay and working conditions; *security* – a permanent contract of employment; *social* – introduce team working; *esteem* – appraisal; *self-actualisation* – offer opportunities for enhancing skills and achievement by offering regular training in new skills.

4 a) salary – hygiene; b) recognition for achievement – motivator; c) relationship with supervisor – hygiene.

Unit 26

Test yourself

1 Feedback is built into the job; the employee is held responsible for checking the quality of their own work; opportunities for a sense of achievement are built into the job.

2 Teams may be more likely to come up with creative ideas by sharing their thoughts on each job. Teamworking may well help to motivate the staff to work more effectively because their social needs are being met at work.

3 The normal and accepted way of doing things within an organisation will be a key determinant as to the level of productivity achieved within the firm. If everyone expects everyone else to work to the very best of their ability then the culture is likely to have a beneficial impact on quality levels too. A strong culture would also help new employees to feel that they know what is expected of them when they join the firm.

4 They may have taken the job simply to make money and

care little for how much decision making power they have. They may lack the experience and skills required to make the right decisions and may therefore become demotivated if they feel they are doing a poor job.

5 a) Sales staff in a fashion clothing retailer: commission may encourage many sales to be made, but some kind of profit sharing based on the branch's profit may produce better overall results for the firm. b) The manager of a branch of a chain of fashion clothing retailers: salary should be used, possibly with bonuses linked to the performance of their branch – probably profit level if the branch is operated as a profit centre.

Unit 27

Test yourself

1 Encourages delegation; improves communication from bottom to top.
2 Wider spans of control will reduce the height of a structure.
3 Benefits: employee knows how the organisation works, you know the employee better and are less likely to make a mistake in selection, other staff feel promotion is possible if the firm regularly recruits internally. Drawbacks: leaves a vacancy unfilled elsewhere in the business.
4 Most = Director; least = Team Leader.
5 Passing decision-making power down the organisational structure.
6 Taylor felt that money motivates people to work and they should therefore be paid piece rate. He felt that the ideal method involves differential piece rates with a higher rate per unit being paid after output targets have been achieved.
7 Training will be specific to the actual workplace, unlike general training.
8 Social facilities can be provided; teamworking would also be effective.
9 Recruitment is the part of the process of getting new staff that identifies the need to recruit, advertises the job and gets candidates interested. What happens then is selection, as the applicants are whittled down to fit the number of vacancies.
10 If hygiene needs are met employees will have no reason to be dissatisfied at work. They will not, however, be motivated unless the motivators are also being addressed.
11 Teamworking will give staff an opportunity to work with colleagues, thereby addressing the need for human interaction at work, as first identified by Mayo. Teamworking should help to address the social needs within Maslow's hierarchy.
12 Piece rate; performance-related pay; profit sharing;

share ownership; fringe benefits; salary.

13 $\frac{\text{No of staff who left work}}{\text{Average total staffing level.}} \times 100$

14 Falling productivity is likely to lead to increased costs per unit, meaning the firm must either increase their selling price or accept lower profit per unit.
15 Falling productivity can be caused by motivation problems or poor equipment or machinery.

SCC Ltd

1 The number of subordinates under the direct control of a manager.
2 High quality trained staff were available from the moment the business opened in each town. Recruiting plenty of staff helped to ensure that the firm could cope with initial demand from the outset, meaning no disappointed customers.
3 Internal training is likely to be much cheaper. It also allows the firm to train staff to do things 'the Mainwaring and Werge way' – helping to reinforce company culture.
4 Delegating more power to local representatives may motivate them a little more and allow them to make changes to the service to suit the local market. However, mistakes here may be very costly and a centralised structure helps to avoid these. Furthermore, a strength of the business may be the standardised nature of the service that they offer – something that may be lost if power is decentralised.

Ramsbottom Engineering

1 $5/80 \times 100 = 6.25$ per cent.
2 Empowering staff clearly encouraged them to put forward their own ideas, based on their skills and experience. It was these suggestions that showed Jackie the way through the tough trading conditions.
3 Staff would become concerned for the safety of their jobs, which according to Maslow would threaten their security needs. If employees have their job security removed they are likely to work less effectively.
4 Jackie's approach seems likely to work well when dealing with similar workforces in similarly sized firms. With just four supervisors this firm must be small enough for all staff to feel a genuine commitment to the firm's goals and be committed to the success of the business. By involving staff in decision making, Jackie has enabled them to share their expertise and experience successfully. However, inexperienced staff may have less to offer or be less willing to offer their views. The established culture within a business can be very difficult to change. Meanwhile larger firms may need to retain certain levels of authority to ensure that coordination is effective.

Unit 28

Test yourself

1 Good customer service meets or surpasses customer expectations of an organisation.
2 Identify customer expectations; design a system to meet expectations; train staff; monitor levels of service provided.
3 *Customer loyalty* – predictable cash flows – makes planning easier.
Word-of-mouth promotion – saves money – increasing profit margins.
4 Any firm for whom price is a key selling point.
5 Lack of training; failure to monitor what service is being provided. Both may be the result of attempts to 'cost-save' by taking short cuts.

Unit 29

Test yourself

1 Quality management is the maintenance of consistent levels of quality.
2 A good quality product is: easier to establish in the market; generates repeat purchases; has a longer life cycle; allows brand building and cross marketing; saves advertising costs; allows a price premium; makes products easier to place. There are also costs associated with poor quality.
3 Inspection of finished goods, for instance at the end of a production line. Self-inspection of work by operatives, at every stage in the production process.
4 Total quality management; continuous improvement; zero defects; quality circles; training; benchmarking.
5 Loss of sales; scrapping of unsuitable goods; reworking of unsatisfactory goods – costs of labour and materials; handling complaints/warranty claims.
6 There is no 'right' level of quality. A balance must be made between cost and the level of quality. A hundred per cent quality is possible but only at a very high price. It may depend on the market: at the cheap and cheerful end lower quality may be more acceptable; at the premium end poor quality will be unacceptable. It also depends on the product. The requirements for food are different to those for clothes. Industrial buyers will demand certain levels of quality to ensure their products are not affected.

Unit 30

Test yourself

1 Reliability; frequency of deliveries; flexibility; payment terms.
2 Increased flexibility with suppliers, which may be especially important in the fashion industry given the speed of new product development required; willingness to work together on new products, since manufacturers will be able to tell Primark exactly what they can and cannot do within the budget that Primark is working to.
3 Fresh products cannot be kept in stock for a long term, meaning daily deliveries may be necessary. Failure to deliver may leave the restaurant needing to tell customers that some items on its menu are not available – never popular with customers.
4 If Tesco do not need to part with their cash until two weeks after the bananas are delivered, they will almost certainly have sold the bananas by the time they must be paid for meaning that they have already received the cash from customers – promoting a very healthy cash flow for Tesco.

Unit 31

Test yourself

1 20,000/25,000 x 100 = 80 per cent.
2 a) £100,000/20,000 = £5 per unit.
   b) £100,000/25,000 = £4 per unit.
3 a) Machinery unused, with staff standing around doing little and possibly large stocks of materials lying around a quiet factory. b) Very low room booking rates with lots of rooms empty most nights, and perhaps an empty restaurant as well.
4 To increase the number of customers using the facility, the leisure centre could run special offers with low entry fees, perhaps encouraging existing users to come more often. A drastic alternative would be to close a part of the centre, perhaps selling off an underused playing field to a housing developer – thus reducing total capacity and, if visitor numbers remained unchanged, increasing capacity utilisation.

Unit 32

Test yourself

1 Missing out on possible revenue, loss of customers who switch to rival bakeries and never come back.
2 Primark will be left with unsold stock of flip-flops. It may need to cut prices to try to shift stock, and end up selling them for less than they cost to make – causing them to make a loss on each pair sold at the reduced rate. Alternatively, stock will need to be thrown away – meaning no revenue is earned at all to offset the cost of making the dumped flip-flops.
3 The firm may wish to hang on to the expertise of staff or the equipment in which it has invested. It may also feel that demand is 'just about to pick up' again and doesn't want to be left short of production capacity.
4 They may still make a small profit on each chicken, meaning the order is profitable; they may use this as a way to convince Tesco to buy from them regularly, thus gaining a new, huge customer; they may have excess chickens that they need to get rid of, just to make a little money on them.
5 They give staff a target to aim for; they give a figure against which performance can be checked to measure success.

Unit 33

Test yourself

1 Reduced design costs and designs should get to the market faster as they can be electronically transmitted to suppliers in the Far East.
2 Production planning and deliveries should be more accurate since they know quicker how much stock is needed to replenish Sainsbury's stores. This is particularly true for a firm that will try to avoid large amounts of finished stocks which will need refrigeration and could go out of date if not sold quickly.
3 Production robots may speed up the production process, increasing productivity and reducing the cost per unit. Robots may also be able to work to a particularly high level of accuracy, thus boosting quality levels and enhancing the firm's reputation.
4 Manual stock control is unnecessary, saving the time and money involved in an employee regularly checking stock levels. Stock levels can be monitored more accurately, reducing the chances of too little stock, leaving some menu items unavailable, or too much stock of perishable products.

5 They can reduce costs by getting rid of call centres for phone bookings. They can also take bookings 24 hours a day which may make them more convenient for customers.

Unit 34

Test yourself

1 Benchmarking is a management tool that involves comparing business processes with those of other firms and incorporating the ideas that make the other firm better in the business processes.
2 A quality circle is a group of workers that meet to discuss quality issues. It contributes ideas to improve the business processes in order to improve quality. This in turn reduces costs. It also improves worker morale by increasing involvement.
3 Increase demand; reduce capacity to meet demand; improve production efficiency to make use of available capacity.
4 Increased output reduces average costs by sharing the fixed costs between a larger output. Purchase savings may reduce variable costs.
5 Poor communication, poor coordination, poor motivation.
6 Job production produces small numbers of items individually; batch production produces batches or groups of identical items.
7 Stock may not arrive in time so slowing or stopping the production process, leading to customers having to wait.
8 Length of the production process and the time taken to get deliveries from supplier.
9 Gives the product a good reputation; encourages repeat sales; makes the product easier to place.
10 Average costs = total cost (fixed costs = variable costs)/units produced. Fixed costs are spread over a larger number of units.
11 Office IT processes help management. Automated production processes speed production, reduce stock, lower defects. Automated stock handling speeds distribution.
12 Flow production is usually the system used as it produces large quantities of identical products at a lower cost.
13 Kaizen is continuous improvement. If it is to succeed it needs: commitment from management, commitment from workers, empowerment of workers, investment in costs.
14 TQM is a change in attitude that requires everyone working in the business to take responsibility for quality.
15 Reducing the levels of stock held means that less cash is tied up in stock. Just-in-time means that

goods go out to customers very soon after material supplies are received, so reducing the time between cash in and cash out.

16 *Advantages*: faster production; less human error; output more consistent; quality and consistency improved. *Disadvantages*: loss of labour skills; cost of machinery; loss of motivation; machinery breakdown.

Online stock management

1 To provide the service to the public by gritting the road when the weather turns icy.

2 An automated stock management system enables the stock levels to be monitored quickly and easily. This means that reordering can be done on time and at the right level.

3 **Content** (2 marks): A computerised production process is where some or all of the production process is controlled by computers. This may range from simple computer-aided systems to fully automated production process such as robotics. **Analysis** (4 marks – 2 for advantages and 2 for disadvantages): *Advantages*: saves time and labour costs; less human error; process can often be speeded up; may be space saving. *Disadvantages*: loss of worker morale as machines do the job; if there is a breakdown it may be time consuming to resolve; cost of investment in systems and machinery; loss of labour skills.

4 **Content** (1 mark): Shows an understanding of what is meant by quality. **Application and analysis** (4 marks): Quality has both costs and marketing implications for the business. (For full marks answer should include one marketing and one cost implication.) In a competitive market poor quality can result in: loss of sales; loss of reputation; may need to reduce prices; may make it difficult to place goods at retailers; loss of goodwill and repeat purchases; may impact on other products in the range. Costs are increased because of: scrapping of unsuitable products; reworking time to correct faults; lower prices for seconds; warranty and complaints costs.

5 **Content** (2 marks): Just-in-time system of stock management means getting required stocks of materials or components, as they are needed by the manufacturing process. **Application** (2 marks): Answer must be focused on the firm in the question and/or related to real life examples that are relevant to the question. **Analysis** (4 marks – 2 for advantages and 2 for disadvantages): Many of the materials for this firm will be provided just-in-time in any case. Fresh ingredients need to be delivered fresh each day. Other ingredients could be stocked. Reduced stock holding will save on costs. It may be difficult to arrange JIT deliveries of all ingredients depending on the size of the firm and its orders and its relationship with the suppliers. Like any other firm using JIT, if there is a problem with suppliers it could affect the production process.

Challenge 50

1 The business is reacting to the situation in the market rather than just producing cars. Production is focused on market demand.

2 **Content** (1 mark): This is a productivity improvement. **Application and Analysis** (3 marks): Use the figures in the table to support this, e.g. fewer defects, fewer inspectors, less stock held.

3 **Content** (1 mark): Benchmarking is a process of comparing against the best in order to improve business processes. **Application** (2 marks): Relate to the business – both are car manufacturers. Suzuki is a world-class car producer – 'best in class'. Use information given to analyse the benefits. **Analysis** (4 marks): As well as improving efficiency and reducing costs it has released floor space allowing them to increase capacity by almost 50 per cent. Contributed to other Challenge 50 improvements.

4 **Content** (1 mark): Kaizen is continuous improvement. **Application** (2 marks): Answer should relate to the information given or use other practical examples. A general answer gets no application marks. **Analysis** (3 marks): *Advantages*: Worker involvement; improvement in production processes; cost reductions at factory and suppliers. *Disadvantages*: Cost of running the scheme; overwhelming number of suggestions. **Evaluation** (2 marks): A judgement about the system for this factory.

Unit 35

Test yourself

1 The business activity that links the product to the customer.

2 Effective marketing will increase profitability by increasing sales. It will enhance the company image and avoid costly mistakes.

3 If a firm is to sell its products it needs to know about the market that it is operating in. If it does not have this knowledge it may be very difficult to sell the product.

4 Marketing will only be successful if it is part of an overall company strategy. Production and distribution need to be fully involved in any marketing campaign to ensure that the product is available. Finance may be required to fund a marketing programme and the commitment of management and workers is essential to ensure the success of marketing activity.

5 Market knowledge; value for money; continuous process; integrated through the whole business.

6 The unethical aspect is persuading them to buy products that will make them fat, if they buy/eat too many. It is the same issue as advertising alcohol: fun to consume moderately, dangerous if consumed to excess.

Unit 36

Test yourself

1 Selling to a wide market.
2 Lower-priced products with consistent quality.
3 Products that are different from other products in the market. They may be innovative or exclusive or just appealing to a small group.
4 To introduce new brands; by breaking down the mass market into smaller segments.
5 i) The company lacks the expertise and the finance to compete with the big, multinational producers; ii) its marketing proposition is based on being small and exclusive.

Unit 37

Test yourself

1 Product, price, place and promotion.
2 A successful mix will produce customer satisfaction and help to achieve the marketing objectives.
3 Probably 'place' would be the hardest to achieve successfully, i.e. obtaining sufficient distribution to give the product a fair chance of building a customer base. Promotion would be necessary to let customers know about the new product. Pricing will be important as there are many alternative products in the market. The product itself must be good or it will not sell.
4 Personal visits by sales representatives, to explain the lorries' special features. Direct mail advertising, e.g. posting catalogues to the relevant purchasing decision makers at each company in the target market.
5 A smaller section of a market for a particular product.

Unit 38

Test yourself

1 A product is something that is offered to the market.
2 Tangible benefits are those that can be measured. Intangible benefits cannot be measured. They include things such as pleasure, satisfaction or peace of mind.
3 Market research helps to understand the customer and the market. Product research concentrates on the product.
4 Businesses use market and product research to tailor products to customer requirements. It will help them to get the right product to the right part of the market.

5 A USP is a feature or aspect of the product that makes it different to rival products.
6 To make the product stand out in the market; to appeal to different target groups; to build brand loyalty and so reduce price sensitivity and make repeat sales.
7 Think about the product itself. Does it have any special features? Think about the packaging. Where the product is sold. Pricing. Is it unique or does it have competitors? If in a competitive market what has made it successful?

Unit 39

Test yourself

1 Development, introduction, growth, maturity, decline.
2 They may be very successful brands with loyal customers. The business may be supporting them or slightly modifying the product to keep it 'fresh'. (In Coca-Cola's case, Diet Coke now outsells Coke in the UK.)
3 By adding marketing support; by modifying the product; by extending the market either to different groups or to different markets.
4 A product portfolio is the list of products that a business is currently making or selling.
5 A tool that is useful in helping firms to analyse their product portfolios. It looks at a firm's brands in relation to market share and the rate of growth in the market sector.
Products are classified in four ways. As *Cash cows*, *Rising stars*, *Problem child* or *Dogs*. The company will want to have a mix of them and will certainly not want to have a portfolio of dogs. It can then think how to adjust the balance of the poorer performing products.

Unit 40

Test yourself

1 Promotion is a general term that covers all of the marketing activity that focuses on letting the customer know about a product and persuading them to buy that product.
2 If the business or product is unknown awareness needs to be created.
3 Market research ensures that the right message gets to the right people.
4 The mix of different types of promotional activity, such as TV advertising, direct selling, mail shots.
5 To ensure that the money being spent on promotion is being effective and is producing the desired results.

Unit 41

Test yourself

1 Products that are readily available will often be priced lower than goods in short supply.
2 Revenue = quantity sold (units) x price.
3 Skimming is used when the product is innovative and there is no competition. The price can be set at a high level allowing the firm to recoup the development costs. Penetration pricing is used when launching a product into an existing market. The price is set lower than that of competitors to gain market share.
4 Firms offer discounted prices for several reasons such as early payment, large quantities purchased, seasonal offers and trade business.
5 A mark-up is added to the average cost.
6 The firm may not recover its costs; customers may think that the product is inferior.

Unit 42

Test yourself

1 Demand for the product is price sensitive. Demand will change by a greater percentage than the percentage change in price.
2 Price elasticity = % change in quantity demanded divided by % change in price
Percentage change in demand = 18,000/120,000 × 100 = 15%
Percentage change in price = 2/20 × 100 = 10%
3 Price elasticity of demand = 15/10 × 100 = 1.5
Product is price elastic.
4 The demand will fall by a greater percentage than the price increase resulting in lower revenue.
5 (a) A price inelastic product – water, gas, designer clothes, specialist hi-fi equipment.
b) A price elastic product – standard brands of lager such as Carlsberg, when sold in a supermarket or off-licence.
6 Improve brand awareness, differentiate the product, add value, lower the competition.
7 Price reduction is 10% (50p/500p × 100). Percentage change in volume = 20% (2 × 10%). New volume = 120,000 (100,000 + 20%).

Unit 43

Test yourself

1 Place is about availability. It includes the physical place, availability and timing. It is where the customer is.
2 Retailers are often unwilling to take a risk. The product is unknown so there may be little or no demand.
3 (a) Travel agents, on the internet, in popular newspapers and magazines.
(b) In small fashion shops, market stalls, internet.
4 Prices may be lower; ease of shopping; promotion by web-based retailers.

Unit 44

Test yourself

1 A market where there are several firms or products trying to get customer attention.
2 A market that is dominated by a few large firms.
3 Making the product stand out from its rivals.
4 The portion of the market that any one firm has.
5 *Design* – a good product that is well designed will attract customers.
Packaging – attractive packaging can get the buyers' attention.
Quality – poor quality products lose customers.
Unique selling point. – having a USP will mark the product out from its rivals.
Brand image – this keeps customers loyal and attracts customers even when there is no real difference in the product.
Lower prices – when products are very similar customers will often use price to make their choice.
Promotion – all forms of promotion contribute to bringing the product to the buyer's attention and hopefully persuading them to buy the product rather than that of a rival.
6 Unless the whole business is cost efficient costs will be high so it will be harder to compete.

Revision checklists

Revision checklist for Unit 1

Can you?

	Very well	OK	No
Identify and/or recognise the qualities of entrepreneurship required for start up success (read *Business Review* 2008: 'Ice Cream Dream' (Sept) and 'Scoop' (Nov)			
Understand 'the market' as a combination of: the customers, the competitors and the distributors, eg the retailers. An entrepreneur must understand all three to truly understand 'the market'			
Understand why many business start-ups fail; and the possible consequences of failure (read *Business Review* September 2008 on 'Zoom Doom')			
Identify the key elements of a business plan and see the problems of obtaining accurate data about the present – and the need for (but impossibility of getting) accurate data about the future			
Evaluate the logic of a business idea: are you willing to question assumptions made by the entrepreneur? Can you judge the idea through logic, not personal prejudice ('I don't like it; I don't think anyone would buy it')			
Evaluate the business plan as a whole, identifying its strong and weak points, then come to a general conclusion about whether it makes a strong enough case			
Understand risk – as a source of adrenaline; as something that must be calculated and evaluated; and as a possible justification for financial reward			
Understand opportunity cost, both as a factor in business start-up and as a concept at the heart of every business decision			
Calculate profit accurately, using revenue, fixed costs and variable costs; also calculate changes in revenue and in profit			
Understand and interpret a break-even chart; indicate the break-even point, safety margin and profit; calculate the break-even point and break-even revenue			
Understand the role of a cash flow forecast within the overall process of devising a business plan			
Distinguish between internal and external sources of finance, and identify sources suitable for short-term and long-term needs			
Understand the difference between limited and unlimited liability and the meaning of the term 'company'; know the sources of finance that are realistic in the context of limited and sole trader start-ups			
Calculate: percentage change (CHANGE/ORIGINAL x 100); total revenue; total costs; profit; break-even; safety margin			
Calculate, understand and interpret data relating to market size (volume and value), market trends and market share			
Understand the importance of market research in keeping the business in touch with customers; outline the meaning of primary and secondary; qualitative versus quantitative; sampling methods; and be aware of causes of bias in research			
Understand small business marketing: the relevant opportunities such as Public Relations, leaflets, local papers; the value of word-of-mouth (free) advertising			
Understand the need to know 'NOW': current trends (as opposed to fads) and current circumstances, e.g. the economy and consumers' willingness to spend; even if it's a great business idea, is it the right idea for now?			

Revision checklist for Unit 2

Can you?

	Very Well	OK	No
Analyse a firm's organisational structure to see whether it is suited to the firm's circumstances and needs			
Measure the effectiveness of a workforce? See the causes and effects of low/high labour turnover and low/high productivity			
Understand the key features of recruitment, selection and training. Distinguish between recruitment and selection. See why some firms recruit for attitude, others for skills			
Understand a wide enough range of motivation theories to be able to analyse different business situations. Recommend: either Mayo and Herzberg or Taylor and Maslow. Do you know how each theory can be turned into business practice?			
Explain how each theory can be turned into business practice. See the role of job rotation, job enrichment and teamworking			
Distinguish between the main ways to manage quality in both manufacturing and service businesses. See the difference between quality targets and a quality culture			
Use the concept of capacity utilisation. Know the determinants, the consequences of under-utilisation and know how to boost utilisation			
Analyse why different firms work so differently with their suppliers. Assess the impact of becoming too dependent on your suppliers			
Identify what parts of the course come under the heading Operations Management and see the dividing line between Operations and People Management			
Show a full understanding of the marketing mix; see how the mix emerges from the marketing strategy. Why is an integrated mix important?			
Understand the different pricing strategies and distinguish them from tactics. Know the right circumstances for different strategies to be used			
Product life cycle and portfolio. Do these models provide 'truths' or 'theories'? How should they be used? How does the Boston Matrix relate to the product life cycle?			
Understand marketing and competitiveness. How do firms achieve a highly competitive position? How can a small firm become competitive against a big rival?			
Analyse a break-even graph and add new lines to the graph to help in making business decisions			
Explain how and why budgets are used. How do firms respond when they suffer adverse budget variances (or enjoy favourable ones)?			
Interpret, adjust and make suggestions for improving a cash flow forecast. Understand the consequences of poor cash flow			
Profit, profit margins and profitability. What is the difference between profit and profitability? What are the main ways to improve profit?			
Are you able to avoid treating cash-in as the same as revenue? And can you explain why cash flow is different from profit?			

Note: page numbers in **bold** refer to keyword definitions.

Index